Philosophy of Religion

John E. Smith

YALE UNIVERSITY

Sources in Philosophy

A MACMILLAN SERIES
Lewis White Beck, General Editor
THE MACMILLAN COMPANY, NEW YORK
COLLIER–MACMILLAN LIMITED, LONDON

I am pleased to have an opportunity to express my gratitude for the valuable suggestions made by my colleague Thomas K. Swing. Also I wish to thank Morris Deane for helping with the preparation of the manuscript. To my wife, Marilyn, I am most indebted of all; her help has been indispensable.

First Printing

Library of Congress catalog card number: 65–11875

THE MACMILLAN COMPANY, NEW YORK

COLLIER-MACMILLAN CANADA, LTD., TORONTO, ONTARIO

Printed in the United States of America

Contents

Introduction

The philosophy of religion embraces a multitude of questions. These questions stem not only from the varied nature of religious faith but also from the many different philosophical perspectives that have been involved in the concerted effort to understand God and the religious life. At times the philosopher's task in confronting religion has appeared to be uncertain and at others skeptics have doubted whether a philosophy of religion is possible at all. There are some at present who hold this latter view, claiming that religious insights are beyond rational comprehension. Attempts, however, at keeping philosophy and religion in separate compartments have never been permanently successful. The claim that religion and philosophy are mutually irrelevant is itself a philosophical thesis. And if such a claim is to be more than a dogma establishing obscurantism by fiat, critical arguments will have to be advanced. The defense of the claim takes us back to philosophy. Exactly how philosophy and religion are to be related is a matter of legitimate concern; that the two have nothing to do with each other is a thesis that cannot be consistently maintained.

Four basic concerns make themselves manifest; they are central to any philosophical treatment of religion. These concerns are: the problem of God, involving both the meaning of the divine idea and the critical discussions dealing with God's existence; the relation between God and the world, including the question of the connection between religion and scientific knowledge; the fact of many different religions and the prospects for genuine encounter between them; the proper relations between religious faith and philosophical criticism, including the role of reason in determining religious commitment.

I. THE PROBLEM OF GOD

Just as the *doctrine* of God is central for religion, the *problem* of God is central for the philosophy of religion. By the "problem of God" we do not mean any single question or issue, but rather a cluster of problems inevitably arising in the encounter between religion and philosophy. What do we mean by God? Does God exist? Can the existence of God be demonstrated? Can we know God through experience? These and other questions are the proper objects of attention when we speak of the problem of God.

1

Of special importance in the development of modern philosophy is the problem of God's reality or existence. The present age has been described as one that has lost God and is seeking to find him again. While the reality of God is the first certainty of the religious man, for philosophers it is the final problem. Philosophers and theologians alike have been forced to pay attention to the doubts that have arisen and the difficulties that must be met if we are to maintain the reality of divinity. Closely related to the question of God's reality is the problem of the divine nature. The two obviously must go together. Just as we would not consider asking whether there are any unicorns without at least a rudimentary idea of what a unicorn is like, we cannot consider whether God exists without possessing some idea of what we are looking for. Whether God is— in whatever form that question may be raised—cannot finally be decided unless we pay attention to *what* or *who* it is we are talking about. Stated in classical terminology, the question of existence (the "that") cannot be treated abstractly, but only in relation to the essence (the "what").

Three major conceptions of the divine nature have made their appearance in the Western tradition of philosophical and religious thought. First, there is the conception of a divine Self transcending the world and interpreted in personal terms; secondly, there is the idea of God as a wholly immanent Order or Power to which all finite reality is subject; thirdly, there is the monistic conception of God as the Absolute or all-embracing totality. The first of these conceptions is found primarily in the Judeo-Christian tradition and in the writings of certain of the ancient Greek philosophers; the second idea is found in such thinkers as Spinoza and some writers in the mystical tradition; the third conception is that of Hegel and of modern absolute idealism. The three conceptions are not mutually exclusive and they have in fact interpenetrated during the long history of Western theological thought. Since there is a measure of truth in all three conceptions, only a view comprehensive enough to harmonize them successfully will be able to maintain itself. Quite apart, however, from the problem of combining the different views is the question of the connection between any one of them and the manner in which we can come to know that God exists or is real. What we understand God to be provides clues to where we shall expect to find the presence of the divine.

The first conception—God as a divine Self transcending the

world—has dominated the Western tradition; most critical approaches to God's existence have presupposed this conception, although there has been considerable disagreement as to whether God is more appropriately understood as Truth, Being, and the Ground of all things, or as the First Cause and the Necessary Being found in the conclusions of the cosmological arguments (p. 32). In either case God appears as a transcendent reality standing beyond both the world and human consciousness. A complete account of the relations between the different conceptions of God and the avenue of approach to the divine existence is beyond our present purpose. The problem, nevertheless, is important, for it is ultimately impossible to indicate the sort of "existence" God is to have unless we have some clear idea about the sort of reality we intend.

At least three characteristic approaches to the problem of God have been developed in the Western tradition: first, the way of critical or rational argument aiming at either an *understanding* of what is believed (Augustine and Anselm) or at *demonstration* (Aquinas) constraining the mind to accept the divine existence and certain attributes; secondly, the *mystical* route eschewing argument in favor of immediate certainty regarding the nature and existence of God through intuition or insight; third, the *negative route* followed by those who either deny the reality of God entirely, or who claim that knowledge of such matters exceeds our powers, or again, by those, like A. J. Ayer, who claim that the term "god" is meaningless and consequently that we can say nothing significant whatever about theological topics. Naturally, there have been variations within each of these approaches. Not all who accept the way of argument have been satisfied with the same arguments. Exponents of the mystical approach have appealed to many forms of immediacy—feeling, intuition, direct experience. Defenders of the negative approach include those who explicitly deny God, those who are cautious agnostics, and various forms of indifferentism.

Within the tradition of rational argument, two chief types of argument have developed—the *ontological* and the *cosmological*. The first starts with the self, our ideas and reflective capacity, and seeks to show that the very idea of God properly conceived and understood leads us to the insight that God must be real beyond our minds and their ideas. Understanding God as "that than which nothing greater can be conceived," Anselm sought to show that such a being must exist, because if it did not we would become involved in a contradiction. His argument takes the form of claiming, *first*, that since to exist is better than not to exist, unless we understand God as existing, we would be conceiving him as imperfect, which runs counter to what we meant; *second*, that the nonexistence of God is inconceivable because it is self-contradictory prima facie to deny existence to "that than which nothing greater can be conceived."

It is now generally agreed that Anselm has two forms of his argument: first, he argues that existence is a perfection and that God conceived as above must possess that perfection and hence must exist; second, he argues that the nonexistence of God is inconceivable or self-contradictory and hence that God necessarily exists. The second form of the argument pays attention to "existence" as a *mode* of being and to the different senses in which different things may be said to exist.

The ontological way of approach does not start with some outer fact or external object, but rather with the mind reflecting on itself and its ideas. It has been called the way to God that achieves its goal by drawing our thoughts away from the world of passing things in order to contemplate the meaning of the divine idea.

The cosmological approach, as the name implies, starts with the existence of the world, or of some particular facts within it or with some feature that the world exhibits in a pervasive way (for example, the orderly arrangement of things). The logical form of this argument is different from that of the ontological. The cosmological approach requires the law of causality or principle of sufficient reason. The form of the argument is as follows: Something (an object, a particular serial order, an idea) is given or acknowledged to exist; every existing thing or feature of the world we encounter must have a ground, cause or reason why it is so and not otherwise; no finite reality (that is, something that comes into existence at a time and is able to perish) is its own ground or sufficient reason; therefore, since something is acknowledged to exist, there must be at least one reality that has its own ground or sufficient reason within itself. Unless there is God or a self-existing being, nothing could become existent at all.

As a rule the proponents of the cosmological argument rejected the ontological argument on the ground that it is circular and that it could be known to be valid only by God. The chief claim in behalf of the cosmological proofs has been that, in starting with existence as given, there is no need to attempt to derive it from concepts alone. On the other side, the defenders of the ontological argument have insisted that to argue from finite, perishable things can never lead to anything other than a finite God existing in the same order as the world of finite things. Moreover, if one holds, as there are good reasons to hold, that the cosmological arguments rest on the basic principle that is behind the ontological argument, the success or failure of the arguments from the world depends upon the final disposition of the argument from perfection. A reformulated ontological argument based on a concept of perfection that allows for change and novelty and upon a defensible theory of real necessity is very difficult to refute, except by invoking positivist principles that are equally difficult to support.

As one might expect, the arguments for God have been vigorously criticized and finally rejected by some as invalid. The grounds, however, for these rejections and the philosophical motives behind them are varied. Some critics have explicitly denied the reality of God in rejecting the proofs, while others in their criticism have meant only to express skepticism about man's capacity to attain knowledge in the theological sphere. Still others maintain a kind of agnosticism, claiming that the term "God" is meaningless and hence that theological statements are neither true nor false because they do not say anything. This position is the one held by Ayer in *Language, Truth and Logic* (p. 54).

In addition to these negative responses, there is the view according to which rational proofs for God are set aside, not because of doubt about the reality of God, but because of the belief that God cannot be approached through the medium of rational argument. The position outlined by Stace furnishes a dramatic illustration of the experiential approach, and while the mystical religion he upholds would not be accepted by all who agree that belief in God cannot be based on demonstration, Stace's general line of thought is typical.

First, Stace's position requires him to agree with the critics of the rational arguments who say that all arguments for God must fail. Secondly, the issue is removed from the sphere of argument entirely on the ground that God's reality is a matter of direct insight. There are thus two distinct spheres of meaning or universes of discourse—the literal, the logical, and the scientific on one side, and the symbolic, the intuitive, and the religious on the other. From within the perspective of one side, the other appears opaque and unintelligible. From the literal standpoint, the rational approach to God is seen to fail; from the standpoint of religion we find that we can neither know nor have anything to do with the world of scientific explanation. There are two realms and no bridge between them. The two spheres, nevertheless, *intersect* at a point and that point is the human consciousness. Though there is an intersection, there is no interpenetration. Neither side can criticize the other because each is wholly true within its own limits. It follows from what has been said that neither side can conflict with the other; man can live in both worlds without contradiction. God can be approached only through the immediate experience of the person; knowing God is more like the intimate understanding shared by friends than like the universal knowledge of mathematics. All attempts to reach God through universal reason are abortive; all attempts to explain the world by invoking God's existence are futile. There is no point of contact between the religious and the scientific standpoints.

The ways of argument and of insight are positive in the sense that they mark out a way that leads to God. The positivist position on the other hand is radical in its opposition to the religious perspective. Positivism means the dissolution of any religious statement purporting to be true. This uncompromising conclusion is supported largely by considerations drawn from the nature of logic and the use of language. The main thesis is that to be true or false an expression must consist of terms that are meaningful; meaningful terms are those that can be verified or exemplified in *sense experience* (the logical connectives—"if, then" "and" "or" etc.—are accorded different treatment). Terms not capable of such verification are without meaning and the compound expressions in which they occur are likewise without meaning. From this it is said to follow that all forms of expression in which the term "God" is found are without meaning and cognitive import.

Any attempt to resolve the problem of God as posed by the three general approaches sketched—the way of argument, the way of insight or immediate experience, and the way of skeptical dissolution —must take the following considerations into account. First, the positivist approach can never be conclusive in its denial of God, partly because it means ignoring crucial differences between the reality of God and that of, for example, a unicorn, and partly because, to be successful, the positivist has to show the *truth* of the claim that the only meaningful terms are transcripts of sense experience. The development of modern positivism shows how very difficult it is to sustain this claim. Second, the clear-cut distinction between the way of argument and the way of experience cannot be defended. This conclusion is suggested by the fact that further analysis of each way reveals points of dependence on the other. Both the ontological and cosmological arguments depend upon experience and tradition for their starting points and for the intellectual framework used to elaborate them. This means that in neither case are these arguments the deliverance of "pure reason" unmixed with a concrete content derived from contact with the world and other selves. The conception of God with which the ontological argument begins is thoroughly dependent upon a way of thinking about God that stems from the Judeo-Christian perspective. This is not to say that logical refinement of the idea plays no part; it is, however, to deny that the idea springs from reason alone. Or again, the cosmological arguments explicitly set out from experience and their use within the context of any one religion requires the *identification* of the God whose existence is proved—the First Cause, the Prime Mover, and the like—with the God of the religious tradition.

If, however, the way of argument veers around to dependence upon experience, the way of experience can be seen to require a similar move in the direction of argument. The appeal to intuition or to immediate experience cannot be sustained without some form of rational support, no matter how indirect. For the question of the *trustworthiness* of intuition inevitably arises, and once this has happened we must either allay our doubts by showing that intuition is trustworthy or we must succumb to the doubts and have done with the way of insight. This means that although intuition or immediate experience may turn out to be essential for any approach to God, it is never sufficient and self-sustaining. The history of mysticism is a history of indirect arguments aimed at showing that insight is trustworthy and that in the sphere of religion we cannot do without it. In view of the mutual involvement of the two ways of approach, it is reasonable to conclude that the problem of God can be solved only through the cooperation of both.

A final consideration concerns the nature of proof itself and the function of reason in religion. We are more aware than we once were of the impossibility of giving certain proofs for propositions purporting to refer to the actual world. (God, it should be obvious, must belong to the actual.) Proof, moreover, even if it were attainable in religion, would still be insufficient because personal engagement and commitment are essential to religious faith, and both involve the total person and not only the intellect. Proof constrains and forces the mind; the question is, can proof enlist the center of the person by the same coercion? The answer is negative; two reasons support this answer. First, proof or rational coercion all by itself cannot lead to love; without love there can be no commitment to God. Second, proof or rational demonstration does not exhaust the role of reason in religion; everything depends upon the sort of meaning through which the rational argument moves. In mathematics, where the key terms are quite clear and the meanings remain quite steady, demonstration is approached, although even in mathematics there are more uncertainties than are dreamed of by laymen. In the religious sphere, the situation is quite otherwise. The meanings of the key terms, "God," "world," "idea," and so forth are difficult to make precise and they cannot be rigorously controlled throughout a process of reasoning. Demonstration cannot be attained, but understanding can. It is possible through critical reflection to lead to conviction; first, by neutralizing the objections and then by clarifying the ideas proposed for our belief by showing their analogues in concrete experience. The role of reason in religion is to lead to understanding, not to proof.

II. GOD AND NATURE

Whether God is distinct from the world, and, if so, precisely how he is related to the world have long been subjects of discussion among philosophers and theologians. Some of the questions posed are these: Is God identical with nature? Is God a part of nature? Can God exist without the world? Can the world exist without God? The general topic concerns not only the meaning of God but our general understanding of nature as well.

The God envisaged by Aristotle, for example, transcended the world and had to be related to a cosmos that was taken as a vast organic system, whereas the God of Newton (also beyond the world) confronted a universe understood as a machine. With the development of modern natural science new issues were brought to a focus. Many ancient and all medieval thinkers had, in their interpretations of the cosmos, taken God or a divine principle for granted.

The new scientific interpretation of nature, however, led many thinkers to question the need for God. Since science was understood mainly as a quest for causal explanations, they came to doubt the need for God as an explanatory principle. To minds bent on recognizing no realities other than those disclosed by the application of the new physico-mathematical method, God in the religious sense could not be real. Although Newton and other scientific men of the seventeenth and eighteenth centuries retained a place for God in their schemes, gradually the sense of incongruity mounted. By the middle of the nineteenth century, largely under the influence of Darwinism, a full-scale struggle between religion and science was unavoidable. To many at the time it seemed that the scientific picture of nature was entirely incompatible with any conception of God whatever.

While it is now clear that much of the struggle was based on misunderstanding and on a refusal from both sides to penetrate to the philosophical issues undercutting the claims of scientists and theologians alike, we are still very far from understanding how a doctrine of God can be harmonized with the contemporary view of nature. It has been argued repeatedly that if one accepts the general scientific picture of things, he cannot consistently believe in God and in the religious view of the world. Posed in this way, the problem is not so much that of showing how God can be related to a finite world of time, change, and development, but rather of understanding why the scientific outlook is supposed to make God superfluous. It will readily be seen that the problem of God and nature has as one of its facets the problem of the divine existence.

Since we cannot hope to pose, let alone solve, all the problems involved, stress will be laid upon but two: first, the tension and opposition between the idea of God as perfect, self-sufficient, and standing in no need of the world, and the idea of God as a creator who brings the world and the creatures into being and who is concerned for the world and involved in it in the sense that he would not be what he essentially is without the world. Second, there is the problem previously mentioned of relating the idea of God to the world disclosed by modern natural science. The basic question is: Is it true that belief in God is incompatible with acceptance of that world picture?

Boyce Gibson (p. 61) has successfully focused the problems raised by the two conflicting ideas of God. The difficulty is an ancient one and it has long been neglected; the emphasis on change, development, and process in modern philosophy has served to bring it into the foreground in recent years. The problem stems, as do all theological problems, from an attempt to express notoriously difficult religious ideas in clear concepts. The tendency of one school of theologians was to conceive God as an absolutely perfect, complete, impassive, and utterly transcendent being in no need of being supplemented by the creation. The contrasting view envisaged God as a creator concerned for the world and for the creatures in it. From the religious standpoint the difference is crucial. On the former view the individuals do not matter, whereas on the latter view their destiny is linked with God in essential ways.

The conception of God as self-sufficient endangers the reality of time, change, novelty, and creativity within the spheres of nature and history. If God is self-sufficient and already perfect in every respect, then the world, including man and his history, can add nothing. Although this way of viewing God would seem to exalt the deity and to safeguard the divine perfection and majesty, it does so at the expense of the creatures. Among the defenders of this view are Aristotle, Plato (although, as Boyce Gibson shows, it is not the only view found in Plato), the neo-Platonists, and many medieval theologians and some of the mystics.

On the other side is the view of God as outgoing, as desiring and aiming at the greatest possible good for the creation and all the creatures in it. The diversity of creatures and their appropriate perfections are themselves expressions of God's goodness. According to one version of this view, reality is a rational system and for everything that exists there must be a *sufficient reason* why it is so and not otherwise. The ultimate ground of this reason is God, that is, the Being who has sufficient reason within his own nature, who framed everything with the aim of producing the greatest possible *good* and harmony among beings. Far from being superfluous, the creatures exhibit the perfection of the divine wisdom and power working in coordination with each other.

Critics of the outgoing God argue that the divine perfection, the fullness of God, is endangered when God is made to regard the creation in such a way as to depend upon it for even an aspect of his being. If God needs the creatures, the objection runs, he cannot be self-sufficient and if this is so, he is not God. So stated, this view would seem to be in absolute contradiction to the other view of God. If God is self-sufficient, utter changeless perfection, the creatures cannot be the object of his concern; on the other hand, if God is essentially related to and concerned for them, changing, developing, imperfect as they are, he would seem to stand in need of something other than himself. The problem is: Which of the two positions more adequately expresses the relation of God to the world? Or are they perhaps both correct up to a point, so that one is needed to supplement the other?

Is there a way of reconciling the two views? The most fruitful possibility is found through reinterpreting the ancient idea of God as Spirit or Life. Whitehead has developed this line of thought and it is becoming increasingly important for contemporary philosophy of religion. By conceiving God as a living unity of experience open to growth and creativity, Whitehead sought to combine the elements of permanence and change—self-sufficiency and relatedness to others—within the divine nature. On his view, God is not static perfection, indifferent to the passing scene. He is, in Whitehead's language, an "actual entity" who affects the course of events through the good at which he aims, and who is in turn *affected by the world* through the novel elements that come into the divine experience as a result of the creative processes taking place among the creatures. From the standpoint of process philosophy, we do not need to choose between the self-sufficient and the outgoing God as if either conception were in itself wholly true; the divine nature must be so conceived as to show how the elements of change and permanence are brought together in the unity of one divine experience.

Whitehead's philosophy is admittedly difficult and his language is often formidable; both obstacles are hard to avoid when we confront a thinker who is trying to say something new. With effort, however, we can come to an understanding of his novel attack on the problem of relating God to the world. The justification of our effort is two-fold: the importance of the problem and the promise held forth by Whitehead's solution.

The first point to be noted is that Whitehead aims at bringing together in one conception the opposing features of God marked out by Boyce Gibson as the "two strands" in theology. As a first step toward the solution, Whitehead distinguishes between the *primordial* and the *consequent* nature of God. In his primordial nature, God is *with* the creation; he conceives the potentialities latent in the natures of things, determining the forms that can go together and thus the results that are possible. Viewed merely as primordial, however, God is not yet understood as fully actual. In short, the primordial aspect of God is but one side of the truth. For the actual we need more than concepts; we need as well feelings, desire, and consciousness. The realization of the divine experience requires, in addition to what things can become, the definite results showing what they do become. Thus Whitehead speaks also of the *consequent* nature of God, by which he means the world becoming objective in God. Each outcome of the processes that make up individual life and the course of the world comes as a *novel element in the divine consciousness*. What happens in the world makes a difference to the totality of God's experience. The novelty does not, however, come neat; it is seen from the perspective of an eternal aim and a divine wisdom that does not change or pass.

Far from being remote, unrelated or unconcerned, God is involved in every happening. The course of development in all things is not an arbitrary or haphazard one; changes lead to definite results and goals are realized, thus bringing new values into existence. On Whitehead's view the *direction* of all processes—their aim at some good—is derived from God's aim, his wisdom and goodness. The divine aim is needed for every temporal advance as a principle directing the outcome. In thus being related to the world of change and growth, God cares for it. As Whitehead says (p. 77), the most adequate image of God is that of the one who cares about the creatures so that nothing of their transitory life is lost. This is clearly no static God who dwells apart.

The other major problem about the relation between God and the world has to do with the consistency of accepting God and the modern scientific world picture at the same time. Various solutions have been offered to this modern version of an ancient difficulty. Science, according to some, has ruled God out; the cosmic system is said to reveal nothing beyond itself and to be sufficiently intelligible without reference to a divine ground or principle. At the opposite pole are philosophers like Leibniz and Whitehead for whom the cosmic scheme is unintelligible without God. For them the reality of God is necessary for the full understanding of everything that happens. A third view has been expressed that stands opposed to each of the others. According to this view God and the world represent two absolutely different orders of being and neither can be derived from the other. This is the position set forth by Stace.

There is no denying the attractiveness of this solution. It takes seriously the problem of God and the human concern for divine ground so completely ignored by dogmatic materialists. Moreover, it seems to free us from dependence on some of the admittedly precarious "reconciliations" between science and religion that have been advanced in the course of modern thought. It enables us, in addition, to escape the intricate problems arising from the attempt to relate God to the world, and above all it permits us to leave out the puzzling questions that confront us when we reflect about ourselves as citizens of both of these unconnected worlds.

Attractive as the foregoing view may appear, it is itself an untenable solution. Man is to be related to both orders and to live at once in the light of the awareness of God and within the confines of the cosmic system. How can we live in two orders that have no intelligible relations to one another? Religion and scientific knowledge cannot be kept permanently in separate containers. Great as the differences between the two may be, it is quite unrealistic to expect us to suppress our questions and doubts stemming from the impact of one upon the other. And this is especially true on the contemporary scene since the modern man takes nature more seriously than he takes either man or God. A religion that does not relate its beliefs to our knowledge of nature cannot long sustain itself.

One final point is worthy of mention. It has been characteristic of the Judeo-Christian tradition to take history seriously and to fight against any interpretation that reduces either nature as a whole or the individual creatures within it to the status of appearance only. Time, change and individuality, therefore, are to be regarded as belonging among the unchallenged realities and hence as falling within the confines of the divine consciousness. If this is so, solutions to the problems discussed in this section are essential. The doctrine of God must be framed so as to allow for the reality of nature and indeed of all finite things. Ultimately, this means that we must seek to show the connection between permanence and change within the unity of God. This problem remains a permanent challenge.

III. GOD AND THE WORLD RELIGIONS

Modern means of communication and transportation continue to narrow the distance between men and between nations. One of the important consequences of this fact is found in the new encounters that are taking place between the world religions, East and West. These encounters are sometimes tragic as is illustrated by the struggles between Hindus and Moslems; others are more constructive as, for example, in the attempts currently being made by Buddhists and Christians to understand the fundamentals of each other's beliefs. Before considering some of the issues involved in specific encounters between diverse religious systems, we must take note of more basic issues raised by the very existence of a plurality of religions. Even if we decide to ignore the many local and ephemeral forms of religion disclosed by anthropologists and historians in order to concentrate on the so-called "high" religions, we are still confronted with five or six major religions. Each has a venerable history made possible through the development of stable institutions and bodies of authoritative doctrines. The fact that men have sought and have claimed to find God in so many different ways and from such a multitude of standpoints raises interesting and important philosophical problems.

First, there is the question whether we may properly speak of *religion* in the generic sense at all. It is often said that although we speak constantly of religion, all we confront in fact is particular religions. This observation has led to the belief that the term "religion" is but a name indicating the fact of many religions. Others have not been satisfied with this conclusion, instead they have insisted that there is a pervasive structure in religion as an aspect of human experience and that this structure is to be found wherever we find religious faith. One of the most common reactions to the discovery that there exists in the world a bewildering variety in religious belief and practice is skepticism about all religion. It is supposed that the history of religion must be a history of human folly, the product of prescientific ways of looking at the world. Such skepticism can be answered not by following the example of the careless or indifferent who would persuade us that "at bottom" all religions are the same, but by painstaking analysis of the data for the purpose of seeing whether the religions exhibit common features.

Wach (p. 85) has shown how religion, viewed from an empirical standpoint, can be described through certain criteria or distinguishing features. He specifies four such features: (1) the reality we are responding to in religious experience is regarded as the *final* or highest reality; (2) the *total* person is involved in the response, which means that we cannot single out some one human capacity such as the emotions or the mind as a special channel for religious insight; (3) the loyalty found in religion is the most *intense* and final sort of loyalty that overcomes and organizes lesser loyalties; (4) wherever there is religion there is a moral imperative of some kind that expresses the *practical* nature of religion. These features lay stress on the experience of the person in religion; others have sought for recurrent patterns in religious systems taken as a whole.

One such pattern was set forth in barest outline by William James in his *Varieties of Religious Experience*. His proposal is noteworthy and in expanded form it provides us with a powerful tool to be used in a philosophical approach to the many religions. We find in every clearly articulated religious system three elements of structure: first, a vision of an Ideal, variously described as Ground, Order, Person, or in the case of the mystical forms, the Divine Nothingness, and this Ideal defines the true fulfillment of man and the perfection of all things; second, there is a critical judgment made in the name of this Ideal upon man and the world as it actually is, and this judgment is intended to disclose in the actual world some defect or flaw that separates present life from the Ideal fulfillment; third, there is a Power—whether it be knowledge, a person, a divine law, a model for conduct—whose function it is to nullify the distorting effect of the flaw and unite man with the Ideal. By means of this structure we can better understand the plurality of religions and make critical comparisons among them as soon as we are able to say in the case of each religion what the Ideal means for that system, what flaw or distortion separates us from the Ideal, and what Power is to overcome the tragic element.

For example, in Hinduism the Ideal is the Unity that is Brahma, the One beyond all finitude and divisiveness, while in Christianity it is the unity of all the individuals in the love of the Kingdom of God. In Buddhism, the main flaw in life as we find it is the boundlessness and inordinate character of human desire, while in Christianity the flaw is located in the rebellious will of man who insists upon making himself into a god. In some forms of Hinduism, the

Power that is to save man is the philosophico-religious knowledge that Brahma and Atman (the self) are one and that the lines of separation between all things are not finally real, while in the Hebraic tradition the saving power is found in the Law or Torah that unites man and God. Unity in the content of these many religions we do not find, but a unity of structure such as is illustrated in these few comparisons makes it possible for us to come to some understanding of what would otherwise be a mass of different ideas and convictions.

The discernment of pattern and structure, however, does not of itself resolve conflicting claims among the different religions, nor does it show the adherents of any one of them how to respond to the challenge implicit in the existence of the others. It is a relatively simple matter to assume the final truth of the religion to which one is committed and to judge all the others to be in error. But a highly intricate problem is not likely to be resolved by so simple an answer. Starting with the assumption that religion is not all folly, certain alternatives present themselves that a sensible person will not try to avoid. Are all the religions equally true in their own terms, but individually incomplete and awaiting synthesis in some super religion that is not identical with any existing at present? Is one of the existing religions true and destined to overcome the others, incorporating some of their features in its own final form? Do all of the religions have the same goal, as some Hindu philosophers believe, so that one may equally well follow any one of them to the same fulfillment? These and other questions are brought into focus by the present situation. They may be raised by those who are without specific religious allegiance as part of an understanding of the modern world, but the poignancy of these questions becomes clear only when they are faced by the actual adherents of the religions in question.

Tillich and Hocking are both concerned with the issues implicit in the alternatives just indicated. Tillich (p. 95) focuses attention on the elements within a religion that tend to work against the acknowledgment of other religions; Hocking (p. 89) seeks to discover the inadequacies and omissions within each of the major religions for the purpose of seeing to what extent the different faiths may supplement each other.

The relation between a religion and the secular society or "world" in which it exists forms the starting point of Tillich's analysis. His first point is that if religion is not to be lost in mere ideas, it must be expressed in concrete form, involving doctrines, ritual, liturgy, and a church institution in some way marked off from secular life. On the other hand, the existence of a clearly defined cult, or "organized religion," presents new problems and obstacles that may even obscure the universal insights of the religion. The more special or "institutionalized" the religion becomes, the more it tends to become parochial and dogmatic, losing creative relations with the secular society in which it exists. For example, if Christianity is to maintain its original belief in a universal God who is neither an idol nor a tribal deity, it must fight constantly against becoming parochial. If Christianity is not to be reduced to the status of a mere cult, it must take seriously and seek to learn from the criticism directed against it both from secular society and the other religions. Tillich's main point is that only when the adherents of each religion are aware of their own universal insights, clarified through criticism and raised above the level of pride in a special cult, will they be in a position to appreciate the universal insights in other traditions.

We may illustrate the point by considering the high place of importance given by Christianity to the idea of personality in its conception of God. Neither personality nor its limitations can be clearly understood unless attention is paid to the impersonal divine. The fact that a religion as powerful as Buddhism, at least in some of its forms, has rooted itself in the impersonal needs to be taken into account by those who make personality the highest concept. Even more basic is the problem raised for the theistic religions by the Buddhist claim that their religion does not require the concept of God. There is clearly a challenge here that cannot be ignored. The situation calls for a mutual exchange carried on in the form of dialogue as Tillich proposes. Information about the world religions, their doctrines, cultic practices, and so on, has been available for some time, but such knowledge by itself does not guarantee that a genuine encounter between religions will take place. That can happen only when internal obstacles have been removed and the adherents of each faith are able to stand outside of their special viewpoints sufficiently to understand their own universal insights and those of other traditions.

There are other facets to the encounter of the world religions. Can there be a world religion and, if so, is it to be achieved by the extension of an existing religious faith? Hocking recognizes the claim of

Christianity to universality in view of the fact that it has established itself across barriers of race, custom and geography. But in view of this claim, Hocking focuses on the comprehensiveness and adequacy of the Christian tradition in comparison with insights and values to be found in the other religions. He considers the virtues of Buddhism, Hinduism and Islam and asks candidly whether Christianity has sufficient resources within itself to become the foundation for a world faith. Hocking finds in other traditions elements of truth not emphasized by Christianity and cases where Christians have not succeeded in embodying their faith in life to the same extent that this has been done in other religions.

Two clear points emerge from these discussions of the world religions. First, in view of the present world situation, it is becoming more and more difficult for the major religions to ignore each other; confrontation of a serious kind is now unavoidable. The day is past when the various faiths can survive with no more than a nodding acquaintance or polite acknowledgment. Second, serious confrontation requires knowledge and a willingness to understand and compare. As long as the need for serious encounter was believed to be a thing of the future, intimate knowledge could be postponed. Such an attitude is no longer possible. The contemporary challenge made by the secular societies of the world to all religions, makes it imperative that each religion seek to understand itself in relation to the others. Parochialism on the part of the world religions may lead ultimately to far less religion in the world.

IV. GOD AND PHILOSOPHY

Under this heading fall many questions. Most are of ancient origin, but the perennial ones have found new forms of expression in contemporary thought. The recital of typical issues would at the same time serve as an introduction to the entire philosophy of religion. Is philosophy as rational inquiry the sworn enemy of religion? Is there an unbridgeable gulf between the so-called God of philosophy and the God of religion? Is there revealed knowledge and how is it related to the rest of our knowledge and experience? What should be the relations between philosophy, religion, and theology? Can religion be given philosophical support and is such support necessary? These are the fundamental questions.

With regard to the relation between theology and philosophy,

Thomas Aquinas gave classic expression to one of the most influential solutions in the Western tradition.[1] The key to Aquinas' solution is found in the distinction between the natural and the supernatural spheres. Revelation is an expression of the supernatural order; reason operates in the natural order. There are truths that exceed the power of human reason and these can be known initially only through revelation. Thus there is a unified, sacred science of theology whose proper object is God; its content is that of revelation. In addition there is philosophical knowledge derived from the creatures by the light of reason. This knowledge is subordinate to that of revealed theology, but, according to Aquinas, there is no conflict between the two because both have Truth as their object and each has its source in God. It is important to notice that while Aquinas admits a natural theology or knowledge of God based on reason, he carefully distinguishes natural theology from sacred theology. Following Aristotle's account of the manner in which a science argues from its first principles, Aquinas concludes that the articles of faith forming the substance of sacred theology are not matters of argument. As established through revelation, these articles are infallible and they do not form the conclusion of any argument. In view, however, of his belief that revelation and reason cannot conflict, Aquinas maintained that objections against infallible truth can always be answered since no objection made from the standpoint of natural reason can be demonstrative against faith.

Where the solution set forth by Aquinas has been accepted, it has been praised for its clear delineation of the spheres of theology and philosophy and especially for freeing philosophy by assigning to it a domain of its own. From other perspectives, however, the question has been asked whether the placing of philosophy neatly within the natural order as over against the supernatural did not in effect disconnect the two and make philosophy irrelevant to the discussion of theological questions. Moreover, Aquinas' claim that, in principle, there can be no conflict between the content of revelation and the deliverances of reason has met with the objection that the question is begged because it is answered in a way that is entirely a priori.

[1] A contemporary exposition and defence of this point of view will be found in Jacques Maritain's "The Nature of Philosophy and of Theology" in Henry W. Johnstone's companion volume, *What Is Philosophy?* (New York, The Macmillan Co., 1965), p. 29.

While the synthesis of Aquinas was accepted as the more or less official position of the Roman Catholic Church, other positions defining the relation between philosophy and religion were developed both by secular philosophers and theologians in the Protestant traditions. Adopting the standpoint of modern idealist philosophy, Hegel arrived at conclusions concerning God and philosophy that are, in some important particulars, the very opposite of those upheld by Aquinas. Hegel believed above all in the sovereignty of reason. He maintained that reason, conceived after the pattern of his own logic, is able to comprehend everything that exists. There is for him no sphere beyond reason. There are indeed spiritual realities such as God and freedom, but they can be known in a rational way and present no obstacle to the progress of speculative thought.

For Hegel, philosophical comprehension represents reason in its highest form. The task of philosophy is to grasp and express in a system of thought the relations between all things and their final unity in one whole. Philosophy does not construct the truth but discovers or discloses it by penetrating into the depths of the subject matter. In the philosophy of religion, for example, we begin with religion as it manifests itself historically. We always begin, as Hegel constantly repeated, with what is actual. We do not attempt to say what religion ought to be or what we wish it to embody; still less do we aim at expressing personal opinions and convictions. Instead, as philosophers, we aim at grasping what *religion shows itself to be* in its actual historical existence, past and present. In the first instance at least we are led to stand outside of the religious standpoint itself in order to view it in objective fashion in an effort to discover its own nature and not what we ourselves happen to think.

Viewing religion from an external point of view, however, is only the first step; it is not the last. As we penetrate more deeply into the subject matter by studying religion in its many forms, we become aware of a peculiar relation between religion and philosophy: the two are in some important sense the same. This is Hegel's distinctive view and it forms the substance of his entire philosophy. Careful interpretation is required if we are to avoid misunderstanding. What does it mean to say that religion and philosophy are the same? Is not religion an affair of faith and does it not require a community bringing together many people under a unity of doctrine? And is not philosophy an inquiry of reason carried on by individuals who may be little concerned for the practical outcome of their thoughts? Hegel would not deny any of the differences that undoubtedly exist between religious faith and the philosophical enterprise. He concentrated instead on the identity of the two. In saying that religion and philosophy are the same he meant that they have the same goal or objective—the apprehension of Eternal Truth or God. Following in the line of the ancient Platonic-Augustinian tradition, Hegel understood God as that Truth which is the basis of all finite truths. As Truth, God is the final goal both of philosophical comprehension and of religious aspiration.

In philosophical thought the mind is elevated above the details of the world and the facts of daily life; in philosophical thought we concern ourselves with the Infinite, and thus with God. Just as the religious man is asked to withdraw himself from exclusive occupation with the things of the world and direct his thoughts to God, so, for Hegel, is the philosopher to look beyond the truths of finite things, including his own private thoughts and opinions, in order to focus attention upon the Truth itself. There is an element of self-renunciation in each sphere.

Hegel denied that philosophical thought and religion are opposed to each other. In viewing the development of Christian thought, he expressed approval of the long tradition of philosophical theology that began with the early Greek Fathers of the Church and continued through the medieval period. He wanted to preserve continuity between religion and reason. With this end in view, he tried to show that there is in the content of religion latent thought that must be made clear and explicit. Philosophy can perform the function of developing this thought and of bringing the religious insight into rational form. If God is the Truth, then we must seek to understand how all finite truths can be known as one from the divine perspective. The difference between religion and philosophy [2] is found in their forms of expression or in the manner in which they grasp the truth. Religion understands God in imaginative and symbolic form —what Hegel calls an "immediate" form of apprehension—while

---

[2] It is important to notice that for Hegel it is never significant to say that two things are the same unless there is also *some* sense in which they are different. Thus, for example, philosophy and religion are said to be the same in the essential sense that each finds its true nature in concern for the same object— God—but the two also differ in other respects.

philosophy seeks to comprehend God through concepts[3] and in a speculative system. The final outcome of Hegel's view was the translation of religion into speculative philosophy.

To many thinkers since Hegel's time it has seemed that his attempt to show the continuity of religion and philosophy led to the disappearance of religion and the elimination of faith in favor of speculative rationalism. The Existentialist revolt in recent philosophy of religion plus the attacks made on philosophy by neo-Reformation Protestant theology have been directed against Hegel's program. Kierkegaard's ironic and often bitter critique of speculative philosophy was made in the name of the existing individual who, as Kierkegaard saw him, is not meant to be a timeless spectator of all truth but an ethical subject who must act decisively in a precarious world. Kierkegaard's existential attack was directed against Hegel. Where Hegel emphasized the detached or objective thinker, Kierkegaard demanded the involvement of the person in the truth he apprehends. Where Hegel stressed universal reason, Kierkegaard wrote in defense of individual passion and ethical obligation. Where Hegel praised philosophical knowledge and the rational comprehension of all things, Kierkegaard attacked speculation and sought to show the inescapability of religious faith.

The heart of Kierkegaard's existential approach to human life can be seen in his treatment of the problem of God. He was fond of saying that God does not exist, but is eternal. To argue about God's existence as if it were a matter of doubt is to misunderstand the meaning of God and reduce him to a finite object. The individual is not to think of God as a theoretical problem to be dealt with on the basis of objective evidence. Instead, the problem of God concerns the meaning and purpose of the individual's life; all depends on the devotion and sincerity with which the individual relates himself to the divine. Kierkegaard thus stands in the tradition of Luther and Pascal for whom faith and devotion are higher than philosophical wisdom. On the topic of God and philosophy Kierkegaard stands as the polar opposite of Hegel. At the present time the main problem is to decide whether Hegel's belief in the continuity of God and

---

[3] The German term *Begriff* is usually translated as "concept", but in order to bring out the peculiar meaning Hegel attached to the philosophical concept as the unity of many diverse elements in one form of Reason, some translators have used the term "Notion" because it is derived from the ancient Greek word that signified the active intelligence grasping the single meaning in many details.

philosophy was a mistake or simply the exaggeration of an insight that has permanent value.

In Whitehead's philosophy we encounter a view of the relation between religion and philosophy that is different from that set forth by either Thomas Aquinas or Hegel. For Whitehead, religion and philosophy are distinct and neither can be dissolved into the other. Religion has to do with the fundamental character and enduring worth of the person, while philosophy has as its main task the discovery of fundamental notions or categories that are required for the understanding of everything that happens. Though distinct in form and function, religion and metaphysics are far from disconnected. Each makes a contribution to the other.

On the one side, religion is in need of what Whitehead calls a "metaphysical backing." This does not mean that metaphysics stands under obligation to "prove" in rational terms the insights derived from religious experience. Philosophy for Whitehead, in any case, is not a matter of proof but of description or disclosure. The need of religion is for rational interpretation. Religious insight may be lost or obscured by the intensity of concern and emotion it engenders. The preservation of religious insight can be assured and its relation to other aspects of our experience made plain if that insight is interpreted through the same categories that are indispensable for the interpretation of every happening in the world. Thus, for example, if we speak of the religious idea of a Kingdom of God, we shall have to know what we are to mean by a community of persons united in a living bond of faith and love; or again, if we speak of God as transcendent and living we shall have to scrutinize our terms in order to arrive at meanings for "transcendent" and "living" that are in accord with our general understanding of the nature of things. The true rational criticism of religion and at the same time its true metaphysical backing are found at the point where the metaphysical description of the universe is seen to be in accord with what is disclosed through religious experience.

The other facet of the mutual relations between metaphysics and religion is the contribution made by religious experience to the data upon which a metaphysic has to be based. No interpretation of the universe can be called comprehensive unless it takes the results of religious experience into account. Whitehead did not allow that the pervasive religious experience of man gives evidence of a personal God. As he expresses it, there is no "consensus" on the point. What we do find disclosed in religious experience is the awareness of a pervasive character in the universe, a sense of permanent rightness in the scheme of things. This awareness running through religious experience receives interpretation in metaphysical terms through the idea of God as the principle of selection, selecting among possibilities and limiting the outcome of processes so that the greatest good is achieved and preserved.

Religion contributes another basic idea to the stock of notions necessary for the interpretation of the universe—the idea of individuality and its worth. In a philosophy dominated by the idea of process and the community of many elements working together, it is essential that some place be made for the value of the individual for itself. Religion focuses on that aspect of things. An organic universe involves us in a doctrine of the interrelatedness of all things and attention falls on the functions performed and the contributions made by an individual element to the successful outworking of some line of development. But what of the individual himself and his value? Religion thrusts the individual into the foreground and leads us to consider the inherent value of the individual in and for himself —in his "solitude" as Whitehead liked to put it. Without religious experience, we would be deprived of this most important insight and our metaphysics would be deficient if it had no place for considering the individual in his own right.

Of special interest at present is Whitehead's critical reservations about the success with which religious truth can be based on historical foundations. Many theologians at present, aware of the attacks that have been leveled at the metaphysical approach to the interpretation of religious meaning, have attempted to shift the basis of theology from metaphysics to history. The claim is that the metaphysical approach is rooted in the outlook of the classical Greek philosophers and that Christianity should abandon it in favor of the approach through history to be found in the Old and New Testaments. While himself sensitive to the contributions of history to philosophy, Whitehead did not agree with those who would abandon metaphysics.

"History," Whitehead wrote, "presupposes a metaphysic," and this means that the interpretation of the past can be carried out only from the standpoint of a metaphysical scheme that is in the present. The point at issue concerns something more fundamental than differences among historians about the interpretation of some particular event in the past. Whitehead is claiming that we cannot approach the past at all until we have given some definite meanings to the fundamental terms in the inquiry, terms such as fact, event, time, history and the more strictly logical notions such as identity, difference, contradiction, and so forth. Thus the approach to religion through history does not free us from the need for a metaphysical backing.

In the final selection in this book I attempt to set forth the dialectical approach to the relation between philosophy and religion. The aim is twofold: on the one hand religion and theology must not be kept in a separate compartment safe from all criticism at the hands of philosophy and, on the other, philosophy must not attempt to shield itself from dealing with those difficult questions about the nature of things and the status of man in reality that have ever been the concern of religious faith. Stated in other language, religion separated from the critical prod of philosophy is constantly in danger of falling into obscurantism and complacency; philosophy untouched by the goad of religion and its concern for the most urgent questions of human life is constantly in danger of formalizing itself and of occupying its time with strictly preliminary questions of method and meaning while neglecting the larger and more difficult questions. The end result is the belief that if reason is incompetent to deal with the speculative issues of philosophy it is surely unable to attack the problems of religion.

From the religious side another development has been taking place that further widens the gap between philosophy and religion. As mentioned previously, many theologians, skeptical of the metaphysical approach to religious issues, have sought to make history the basis of their discipline and a sharp distinction has been made between the speculative or philosophical approach characteristic of the Greek traditions, and the historical or existential orientation of biblical religion. In this vein, theologians like Karl Barth and others have attacked philosophical reason as incompetent in the sphere of theology and have attempted to construct a purely biblical or dogmatic theology free of all philosophical influence. From this standpoint, moreover, the philosophy of religion is also rejected on the ground that it deals with religion merely in generic terms that are irrelevant for Christianity because the latter is *sui generis* and not to be included as one religion among others in the general category of religion.

The final selection expresses an attack upon this divorce and it represents an attempt at bringing the two sides back into communication by showing their mutual involvement. There is no thought of reducing one to the other or of making one the handmaid of the other. The aim is chiefly to recover the creative encounter that is possible between them. For if philosophy and religion have no point of contact with each other, it is futile to speak of the philosophy of religion.

PART I

The Problem of God

The Ontological Argument

Anselm of Canterbury was born in Aosta in 1033 and entered the Abbey of Le Bec at the age of thirty. In 1093 he was made Archbishop of Canterbury. During his years in the abbey he wrote the two works for which he is best known, The Monologium and The Proslogium. Anselm's name will forever be associated with the Ontological Argument for the existence of God. This argument has been the subject of more discussion than any other single piece of reasoning in the history of Western thought. The argument has often been "refuted," but it has a peculiar power of survival. Anselm's formula of "faith seeking understanding" has provided one of the permanent models for expressing the proper relation between theology and philosophy. Anselm died in 1109.

Truly there is a God, although the fool hath said in his heart,
There is no God.

And so, Lord, do thou, who dost give understanding to faith, give me, so far as thou knowest it to be profitable, to understand that thou art as we believe; and that thou art that which we believe. And, indeed, we believe that thou art a being than which nothing greater can be conceived. Or is there no such nature, since the fool hath said in his heart, there is no God? (Psalms xiv. 1). But, at any rate, this very fool, when he hears of this being of which I speak—a being than which nothing greater can be conceived—understands what he hears, and what he understands is in his understanding; although he does not understand it to exist.

For, it is one thing for an object to be in the understanding, and another to understand that the object exists. When a painter first conceives of what he will afterwards perform, he has it in his understanding, but he does not yet understand it to be, because he has not yet performed it. But after he has made the painting, he both has it in his understanding, and he understands that it exists, because he has made it.

Hence, even the fool is convinced that something exists in the

From St. Anselm, The Proslogium, trans. S. N. Deane (Chicago: Open Court Publishing Co., 1903, pp. 7–10, Chaps. 2–4).

understanding, at least, than which nothing greater can be conceived. For, when he hears of this, he understands it. And whatever is understood, exists in the understanding. And assuredly that, than which nothing greater can be conceived, cannot exist in the understanding alone. For, suppose it exists in the understanding alone: then it can be conceived to exist in reality; which is greater.

Therefore, if that, than which nothing greater can be conceived, exists in the understanding alone, the very being, than which nothing greater can be conceived, is one, than which a greater can be conceived. But obviously this is impossible. Hence, there is no doubt that there exists a being, than than which nothing greater can be conceived, and it exists both in the understanding and in reality.

God cannot be conceived not to exist.—God is that, than which nothing greater can be conceived.—That which can be conceived not to exist is not God.

And it assuredly exists so truly, that it cannot be conceived not to exist. For, it is possible to conceive of a being which cannot be conceived not to exist; and this is greater than one which can be conceived not to exist. Hence, if that, than which nothing greater can be conceived, can be conceived not to exist, it is not that, than which nothing greater can be conceived. But this is an irreconcilable contradiction. There is, then, so truly a being than which nothing greater can be conceived to exist, that it cannot even be conceived not to exist; and this being thou art, O Lord, our God.

So truly, therefore, dost thou exist, O Lord, my God, that thou canst not be conceived not to exist; and rightly. For, if a mind could conceive of a being better than thee, the creature would rise above the Creator; and this is most absurd. And, indeed, whatever else there is, except thee alone, can be conceived not to exist. To thee alone, therefore, it belongs to exist more truly than all other beings, and hence in a higher degree than all others. For, whatever else exists does not exist so truly, and hence in a less degree it belongs to it to exist. Why, then, has the fool said in his heart, there is no God (Psalms xiv. 1), since it is so evident, to a rational mind, that thou dost exist in the highest degree of all? Why, except that he is dull and a fool?

How the fool has said in his heart what cannot be conceived.—A thing may be conceived in two ways: (1) when the word signifying it is conceived;

(2) when the thing itself is understood. As far as the word goes, God can be conceived not to exist; in reality he cannot.

But how has the fool said in his heart what he could not conceive; or how is it that he could not conceive what he said in his heart? since it is the same to say in the heart, and to conceive.

But, if really, nay, since really, he both conceived, because he said in his heart; and did not say in his heart, because he could not conceive; there is more than one way in which a thing is said in the heart or conceived. For, in one sense, an object is conceived, when the word signifying it is conceived; and in another, when the very entity, which the object is, is understood.

In the former sense, then, God can be conceived not to exist; but in the latter, not at all. For no one who understands what fire and water are can conceive fire to be water, in accordance with the nature of the facts themselves, although this is possible according to the words. So, then, no one who understands what God is can conceive that God does not exist; although he says these words in his heart, either without any, or with some foreign signification. For God is that than which a greater cannot be conceived. And he who thoroughly understands this, assuredly understands that this being so truly exists, that not even in concept can it be non-existent. Therefore, he who understands that God so exists, cannot conceive that he does not exist.

I thank thee, gracious Lord, I thank thee; because what I formerly believed by thy bounty, I now so understand by thine illumination, that if I were unwilling to believe that thou dost exist, I should not be able not to understand this to be true.

The Cosmological Argument

Thomas Aquinas was born in 1225 near Aquino in Italy. He joined the Dominican Order in 1244 and several years later became a student of Albert the Great. Thomas taught theology in Paris from 1256 until 1272, except for several years during which he taught at Rome and other cities. He is generally regarded as the most comprehensive of all Scholastic thinkers. His vast Summa Theologica *in which he both distinguished and united philosophy and theology continues to serve as a model for Christian theology within the Roman Catholic Church. Using basic doctrines of Aristotle, Thomas created a monumental synthesis of Christian and Greek thought. He also completed a* Summa Contra Gentiles *in which he attempted to answer the objections brought against Christian faith in the name of reason. He died in 1274.*

THIRD ARTICLE
WHETHER GOD EXISTS?

We proceed thus to the Third Article:—

Objection 1. It seems that God does not exist; because if one of two contraries be infinite, the other would be altogether destroyed. But the word 'God' means that He is infinite goodness. If, therefore, God existed, there would be no evil discoverable; but there is evil in the world. Therefore God does not exist.

Obj. 2. Further, it is superfluous to suppose that what can be accounted for by a few principles has been produced by many. But it seems that everything we see in the world can be accounted for by other principles, supposing God did not exist. For all natural things can be reduced to one principle, which is nature; and all voluntary things can be reduced to one principle, which is human reason, or will. Therefore there is no need to suppose God's existence.

On the contrary, It is said in the person of God: *I am Who am* (Exod. iii. 14).

I answer that, The existence of God can be proved in five ways.

From St. Thomas Aquinas, *Summa Theologica,* Part I, Q. 2, Art. 3, trans. Fathers of the English Dominican Province (London: Burns Oates & Washburn, Ltd, 1920), Vol. I, pp. 19–27. Used by permission of Burns & Oates Ltd, London, and of Benziger Brothers, Inc., New York.

The first and more manifest way is the argument from motion. It is certain, and evident to our senses, that in the world some things are in motion. Now whatever is in motion is put in motion by another, for nothing can be in motion except it is in potentiality to that towards which it is in motion; whereas a thing moves inasmuch as it is in act. For motion is nothing else than the reduction of something from potentiality to actuality. But nothing can be reduced from potentiality to actuality, except by something in a state of actuality. Thus that which is actually hot, as fire, makes wood, which is potentially hot, to be actually hot, and thereby moves and changes it. Now it is not possible that the same thing should be at once in actuality and potentiality in the same respect, but only in different respects. For what is actually hot cannot simultaneously be potentially hot; but it is simultaneously potentially cold. It is therefore impossible that in the same respect and in the same way a thing should be both mover and moved, *i.e.*, that it should move itself. Therefore, whatever is in motion must be put in motion by another. If that by which it is put in motion be itself put in motion, then this also must needs be put in motion by another, and that by another again. But this cannot go on to infinity, because then there would be no first mover, and, consequently, no other mover; seeing that subsequent movers move only inasmuch as they are put in motion by the first mover; as the staff moves only because it is put in motion by the hand. Therefore it is necessary to arrive at a first mover, put in motion by no other; and this everyone understands to be God.

The second way is from the nature of the efficient cause. In the world of sense we find there is an order of efficient causes. There is no case known (neither is it, indeed, possible) in which a thing is found to be the efficient cause of itself; for so it would be prior to itself, which is impossible. Now in efficient causes it is not possible to go on to infinity, because in all efficient causes following in order, the first is the cause of the intermediate cause, and the intermediate is the cause of the ultimate cause, whether the intermediate cause be several, or one only. Now to take away the cause is to take away the effect. Therefore, if there be no first cause among efficient causes, there will be no ultimate, nor any intermediate cause. But if in efficient causes it is possible to go on to infinity, there will be no first efficient cause, neither will there be an ultimate effect, nor any intermediate efficient causes; all of which is plainly false. Therefore it is necessary to admit a first efficient cause, to which everyone gives the name of God.

The third way is taken from possibility and necessity, and runs thus. We find in nature things that are possible to be and not to be, since they are found to be generated, and to corrupt, and consequently, they are possible to be and not to be. But it is impossible for these always to exist, for that which is possible not to be at some time is not. Therefore, if everything is possible not to be, then at one time there could have been nothing in existence. Now if this were true, even now there would be nothing in existence, because that which does not exist only begins to exist by something already existing. Therefore, if at one time nothing was in existence, it would have been impossible for anything to have begun to exist; and thus even now nothing would be in existence—which is absurd. Therefore, not all beings are merely possible, but there must exist something the existence of which is necessary. But every necessary thing either has its necessity caused by another, or not. Now it is impossible to go on to infinity in necessary things which have their necessity caused by another, as has been already proved in regard to efficient causes. Therefore we cannot but postulate the existence of some being having of itself its own necessity, and not receiving it from another, but rather causing in others their necessity. This all men speak of as God.

The fourth way is taken from the gradation to be found in things. Among beings there are some more and some less good, true, noble, and the like. But 'more' and 'less' are predicated of different things, according as they resemble in their different ways something which is the maximum, as a thing is said to be hotter according as it more nearly resembles that which is hottest; so that there is something which is truest, something best, something noblest, and, consequently, something which is uttermost being; for those things that are greatest in truth are greatest in being, as it is written in *Metaph*. ii. Now the maximum in any genus is the cause of all in that genus; as fire, which is the maximum of heat, is the cause of all hot things. Therefore there must also be something which is to all beings the cause of their being, goodness, and every other perfection; and this we call God.

The fifth way is taken from the governance of the world. We see that things which lack intelligence, such as natural bodies, act for an end, and this is evident from their acting always, or nearly always, in the same way,˴so as to obtain the best result. Hence it is plain that not fortuitously, but designedly, do they achieve their end. Now whatever lacks intelligence cannot move towards an end, unless it be directed by some being endowed with knowledge and intelligence; as the arrow is shot to its mark by the archer. Therefore some intelligent being exists by whom all natural things are directed to their end; and this being we call God.

Reply Obj. 1. As Augustine says (*Enchir.* xi.): *Since God is the highest good, He would not allow any evil to exist in His works, unless His omnipotence and goodness were such as to bring good even out of evil.* This is part of the infinite goodness of God, that He should allow evil to exist, and out of it produce good.

Reply Obj. 2. Since nature works for a determinate end under the direction of a higher agent, whatever is done by nature must needs be traced back to God, as to its first cause. So also whatever is done voluntarily must also be traced back to some higher cause other than human reason or will, since these can change and fail; for all things that are changeable and capable of defect must be traced back to an immovable and self-necessary first principle, as was shown in the body of the *Article.*

C. D. BROAD

The Existence of God

C. D. Broad was born in London in 1887 and was educated at Cambridge University. He became a Fellow of Trinity College there and later was appointed Knightbridge Professor of Moral Philosophy. Broad was written extensively on many philosophical topics although it would be difficult to identify his position with a label. In keeping with the Cambridge tradition of preserving a close connection between philosophy and the findings of the sciences, Broad has never accepted the view that philosophy is but the analysis of language or the beliefs of common sense. Broad has long been interested in the mind-body problem, as is shown by his well known book, Mind and Its Place in Nature (1925). In that work he surprised many by taking seriously the investigations of psychical research. Among his many writings are Perception, Physics and Reality (1914), Scientific Thought (1923), Five Types of Ethical Theory (1930), Ethics and the History of Philosophy (1952).

The Ontological Argument. This argument presupposes the notion of degrees of 'reality' or 'perfection'. This notion is never clearly defined, but it seems to amount roughly to the following. A would be said to have 'more reality' or 'a higher degree of perfection' than B, if either of the two following conditions were fulfilled. (i) A has all the positive powers and qualities which B has and, in addition it has some which B lacks. (When this condition is fulfilled we will say that A is *extensively* superior to B'. (ii) A is either extensively equal or extensively superior to B; some of the positive qualities or powers which are common to both are present in A with a higher degree of intensity than in B; and none of them are present in B with a higher degree of intensity than in A. (When this condition is fulfilled we will say that A is *intensively* superior to B'.)

Now the first thing to notice is that these two criteria do not allow us, even in theory, to arrange everything in a single scale of perfection. Plainly the following cases are logically possible. (i) It might be that A has some powers or qualities which B lacks, and

From C. D. Broad, "Arguments for the Existence of God," in *Religion, Philosophy and Psychical Research* (London: Routledge & Kegan Paul, Ltd.).

that *B* has some which *A* lacks. Cats, e.g., can climb trees, whilst dogs cannot; but dogs can track by scent, whilst cats cannot. In that case *A* is neither extensively superior, nor equal, nor inferior, to *B*. Now the criterion for intensive superiority presupposes extensive equality or superiority between the terms to be compared. Therefore, in the case supposed, there can be no comparison between *A* and *B* in respect of either extensive or intensive perfection. (ii) *A* might be extensively superior to *B* and intensively inferior. (iii) *A* and *B* might be extensively equal. But some of their common powers or qualities might be present in *A* with greater intensity than in *B*, whilst others of them might be present in *B* with greater intensity than in *A*. Let us suppose, e.g., that the minds of any two human beings are extensively equal. How are we to compare, in respect of intensive perfection, a mathematical genius of very slight musical capacity with a musical genius of very slight mathematical capacity?

These considerations are highly relevant to the Ontological Argument; for it uses the phrase 'most perfect being', and it presupposes that this is not meaningless verbiage like the phrase 'greatest integer'. In accounts of the Ontological Argument one finds the phrase 'most perfect being' translated in two different ways, one comparative and the other positive. The comparative interpretation makes it equivalent to the phrase 'a being such that nothing more perfect than it is logically possible'. The positive interpretation makes it equivalent to the phrase 'a being which has all positive powers and qualities to the highest possible degree'. Now, as Leibniz noted, it becomes very important at this point to consider whether all positive characteristics are mutually compatible, i.e. whether it is possible for them all to co-inhere in a common subject. Let us consider how this affects the two interpretations of the phrase 'most perfect being'.

(i) Evidently, unless all positive characteristics are mutually compatible, the positive interpretation becomes meaningless verbiage. Suppose, e.g., that it is impossible for an extended substance to be conscious and impossible for a conscious substance to be extended, then it is impossible that there should be a substance which has all the positive properties that there are. The phrase 'a being which has all positive powers and qualities' would be meaningless verbiage like the phrase 'a surface which is red and blue all over at the same time'.

(ii) How would the comparative interpretation of the phrase 'most perfect being' fare on the same supposition, viz. that not all positive properties are compatible with each other? Let us suppose, e.g., that there were just three positive properties X, Y, and Z; that any two of them are compatible with each other; but that the presence of any two excludes the remaining one. Then there would be *three* possible beings, viz. one which combines X and Y, one which combines Y and Z, and one which combines Z and X, *each* of which would be such that nothing extensively superior to it is logically possible. For the only kind of being which would be extensively superior to any of these would be one which had all three properties, X, Y, and Z; and, by hypothesis, this combination is logically impossible. Moreover, these three beings, each of which answers to the comparative definition of a 'most perfect being' so far as concerns extensive perfection, would be incomparable with each other in this respect. For, if you take any two of them, e.g., XY and YZ, each has a positive property which the other lacks. Now the Ontological Argument talks, not merely of 'most perfect beings', but of '*the* MOST PERFECT BEING'. It is now plain that, unless all positive properties be compatible with each other, this phrase is just meaningless verbiage like the phrase 'the greatest integer'.

(iii) Let us now make the opposite supposition, viz. that all positive properties are mutually compatible. Then it is easy to see that nothing could answer to the comparative definition of 'most perfect being' unless it answered to the positive definition of that phrase. For consider any substance which had some but not all of the positive properties. Since all positive properties are now assumed to be compatible with each other, it is logically possible that there should be a substance which should have all the properties which the one under consideration *has,* together with the remaining ones which it *lacks.* This would be extensively superior to the one under consideration, and therefore the latter would not answer to the comparative definition of a 'most perfect being'.

(iv) I have now shown (*a*) that the phrase 'the most perfect being' is meaningless unless all positive properties be compatible with each other; and (*b*) that, if they be all mutually compatible, nothing could answer to the comparative interpretation of the phrase unless it answered to the positive interpretation thereof. The next point to notice is that, even if all positive properties be mutually compatible, the phrase 'most perfect being' may still be meaningless verbiage. For we have now to attend to that part of the positive interpretation of the phrase which we have hitherto ignored, viz. that each positive property is to be present in the highest possible degree. Now this will be meaningless verbiage unless there is some *intrinsic* maximum or upper limit to the possible intensity of every positive property which is capable of degrees. With some magnitudes this condition is fulfilled. It is, e.g., logically impossible that any proper fraction should exceed the ratio 1/1; and again, on a certain definition of 'angle', it is logically impossible for any angle to exceed four right angles. But it seems quite clear that there are other positive properties, such as length or temperature or pain, to which there is no intrinsic maximum or upper limit of degree.

For these reasons it seems to me fairly certain that the Ontological Argument is wrecked before ever it leaves port. However, we will waive these objections and consider the argument itself. I will try to state it as plausibly as I can. It might be put as follows: 'Anything that lacked existence would lack a positive property which it might conceivably have had. Nothing which lacked a positive property which it might conceivably have had would be a most perfect being; for it is logically possible that there should be something superior to it, viz. a being which resembled it in all other respects but had the additional property of existence. Therefore no most perfect being would lack existence. Therefore all most perfect beings exist.'

Let us now consider this argument. It has two steps, viz. a syllogism followed by an immediate inference. There is nothing wrong with the syllogism in respect of its verbal form. It is verbally of the form 'Anything that lacked P would lack M. Nothing that lacked M would be S. Therefore no S would lack P.' This breaks none of the rules; it is in fact a slightly disguised form of the valid fourth-figure syllogism *Camenes*. The second step looks like a generally accepted form of immediate inference, viz. Obversion. But at this point there is a serious risk of a fallacy. The verbal form 'All S is P' is ambiguous. It may mean simply 'If anything were S it would be P', or, what is equivalent, 'Anything that was S would be P'. Interpreted in this way, it leaves the question whether anything *in fact is* S quite open. We will call this the 'conditional' interpretation. On the other hand, it is much more often taken to mean 'There are some S's and none of them lack P'. This may be called the 'instantial' interpretation. Now it is a general principle of logic that it is always illegitimate to draw an instantial conclusion from premises which are wholly conditional. Let us now apply these principles to the second step of the argument.

The two premisses of the syllogism are purely conditional. Therefore the conclusion must be interpreted purely conditionally if the syllogism is to be valid. So the conclusion of the syllogism must be taken to be 'If anything were a most perfect being it would not lack existence'. Now all that can be legitimately inferred from this by obversion is the conditional proposition 'If anything were a most perfect being it would exist'. If you interpret the sentence 'All most perfect beings exist' in this way, the conclusion follows from the premisses but is completely trivial and useless. If, on the other hand, you interpret it instantially, i.e. take it to mean 'There are most perfect beings and none of them lack existence', there are two fatal criticisms to be made. (i) You are attempting to draw an instantial conclusion from purely conditional premisses and therefore are committing a logical fallacy. (ii) The sentence as a whole is pleonastic. It is idle to add 'none of them lack existence' to 'there are so-and-so's', whether the so-and-so's be most perfect beings or potatoes or dragons.

Let us now consider the syllogism itself. As I have said, it is correct in verbal form. Nevertheless, as I shall now proceed to show, it is radically vicious. Its defect is, not that its premisses are false, but that they are meaningless. They are sentences which seem, from their verbal for, to express propositions; but in fact they express nothing whatever. The argument presupposes that existence is a quality or power, like extension or consciousness or life; it assumes that there is sense in talking of a comparison between a non-existent term and an existent term; and it produces the impression that this is like comparing two existing terms, e.g., a corpse and a living organism, one of which lacks life and the other of which has it.

Now all this is nonsensical verbiage. It is intelligible to make a *categorical* comparison between two actual existents, e.g., Hitler and Stalin, in respect of their qualities and powers. It is intelligible to take a description of a merely possible existent, e.g., a creature with a horse's body and a man's head, and to make a *conditional* comparison with an actual existent. It is, e.g., intelligible to say 'If a centaur existed (or, if there were a centaur), it would be swifter than any actual man and more rational than any actual horse'. Lastly, it is intelligible to take descriptions of two merely possible existents, and to make a doubly conditional comparison. It is, e.g., intelligible to say 'If centaurs existed and unicorns existed (or, if there were centaurs and unicorns), the former would be superior (or inferior) to the latter in such and such respects'. Now the Ontological Argument professes to make a *categorical* comparison between a non-existent and an existent in respect of the presence or absence of *existence*. The objection is twofold. (i) No comparison can be made between a non-existent term and anything else except on the hypothesis that it exists. And (ii) on this hypothesis it is meaningless to compare it with anything in respect of the presence or absence of *existence*.

It is evident, then, that the Ontological Argument must be rejected. Probably most people feel that there is something wrong with it; but the important and interesting and not too easy task is to put one's finger on the precise points at which it goes wrong. When a fallacious argument has seemed cogent to many people of the highest intelligence, such as St. Anselm, Descartes, and Leibniz, it is desirable to supplement the refutation of it by an attempt to explain the causes of its plausibility. I believe that there are two causes, in the present case; and I will now proceed to exhibit them.

(i) The first and most important cause of the illusion is the fact that existential propositions and characterizing propositions are expressed by sentences which have the same grammatical form. Thus, e.g., existential propositions are expressed by such sentences as 'S exists' or 'S is real', while characterizing propositions are expressed by such grammatically similar sentences as 'S eats' or 'S is red'. This linguistic fact tempts people to assume uncritically that existential propositions are *logically* of the same form as characterizing propositions. This uncritical assumption makes the Ontological Argument seem plausible. But it is certainly false, as can easily be shown. The demonstration of this fact may be put as follows.

Let us begin with the two negative propositions *Cats do not bark* and *Dragons do not exist*. It is obvious that the first is about cats. But, if the second be true, it is certain that it cannot be about dragons; for there will be no such things as dragons for it to be about. The first might be expressed, on the conditional interpretation, by the sentence 'If there were any cats, none of them would bark'. On the instantial interpretation it might be expressed by the sentence 'There are cats, and none of them bark'. Suppose you try to express the negative existential proposition in the same way. On the first alternative it would be expressed by the sentence 'If there were any dragons, none of them would exist'. On the second alternative it would be expressed by the sentence 'There are dragons, and none of them exist'. Both these sentences are self-contradictory and meaningless. So, if you try to analyse negative existential propositions in the same way as negative characterizing propositions, you will find that they are all self-contradictory. But it is plain that *Dragons do not exist* is *not* self-contradictory. It is not only logically possible but is almost certainly true.

Now consider the two affirmative propositions *Cats scratch* and *Cats exist*. On the conditional interpretation the former would be expressed by the sentence 'If there were any cats, none of them would fail to scratch'. On the instantial interpretation it would be expressed by the sentence 'There are cats, and none of them fail to scratch'. Suppose you try to express the affirmative existential proposition in the same way. On the first alternative it would be expressed by the sentence 'If there were any cats, none of them would fail to exist'. On the second alternative it would be expressed by the sentence 'There are cats, and none of them fail to exist'. Now both these sentences are mere platitudes. So, if you try to analyse affirmative existential propositions in the same way as affirmative characterizing propositions, you will find that they are all platitudes. But it is plain that *Cats exist* is not a mere platitude. It is a substantial proposition which might very well be doubted by a person who had never seen a cat. So it is certain that existential propositions need a different kind of analysis.

The right analysis, as is now well known, is somewhat as follows. These propositions are not about cats or dragons, i.e. about *things* which have the cat-characteristics or the dragon-characteristics. They are about these *characteristics* themselves. What they assert is that these characteristics do apply to something or that they do not apply to anything, as the case may be. 'Cats exist' is equivalent to 'The defining characteristics of the word "cat" apply to something'. Again 'Dragons do not exist' is equivalent to 'The defining characteristics of the word "dragon" do not apply to anything'. Suppose, e.g., that a 'dragon' is defined as a reptile which flies and breathes fire. Then the statement that dragons do not exist is equivalent to the statement that nothing combines the three properties of being a reptile, of flying, and of breathing fire. Such statements are neither tautologies nor contradictions.

It only remains to apply this analysis to statements about the existence or non-existence of a most perfect being. To say that a most perfect being exists is equivalent to saying that something has all positive characteristics to the highest possible degree. For reasons which I have given, it seems likely that this is not only false but also self-contradictory and nonsensical. To say that a most perfect being does not exist is equivalent to saying that nothing has all positive characteristics to the highest possible degree. For the same reasons it seems likely that this is not only true but a truism.

(ii) I strongly suspect that another linguistic fact about the use of the word 'exist' has helped to make the Ontological Argument seem evident truth instead of meaningless nonsense. It is not uncommon to say, of a person or animal who has died, that he has 'ceased to exist'. Now in this case there is something visible and tangible left, viz. the corpse, which can be compared with the person or animal as he was before he died. Moreover, it is obvious that a living organism is more perfect than a corpse. This leads people to think of existence as a positive characteristic which can be added to or subtracted from a thing, and whose presence makes a thing more perfect than it would have been without it. But, in the sense of 'existence' required for the Ontological Argument, a corpse exists as much as a living organism. So this linguistic fact does nothing to *justify* the speculations which it *encourages*.

(1·2) *The Cosmological Argument.* This argument goes back, historically, to a physical argument of Aristotle's about motion. Aristotle's attempt to prove that there must be an unmoved cause of motion is of considerable interest, but, for the present purpose, it seems more profitable to consider the argument in a less specialized form. It may be put as follows.

It starts with the premiss that there are particular things, persons, events, etc. Each of us, e.g., can take himself as an indubitable instance of a particular person and can take any one of his present experiences as an indubitable instance of a particular event. Now any thing or person begins to exist at a particular time and place, lasts for a longer or shorter period, and then ceases to exist. Similarly, any event in the history of a thing or person begins at a certain time. Now the coming into existence of a thing or person of such and such a kind at a certain time and place is felt to need explanation. Similarly, the occurrence, at a certain date in the history of a thing or person, of a change of such and such a kind is felt to need explanation. The first move is to try to explain it by reference to previously existing things or persons (such as parents) and by reference to earlier events. We will call this 'explanation in terms of ordinary causation'. Now this kind of explanation is, in one respect, never completely satisfactory. This is for two reasons. The first is that such explanations always involve a reference to *general laws* as well as to particular things, persons, and events. Now the general laws are themselves just brute facts, with no trace of self-evidence or intrinsic necessity about them. The second and more obvious reason is the following. The earlier things, persons, and events, to which you are referred by explanation in terms of ordinary causation, stand in precisely the same need of explanation as the thing or person or event which you set out to explain. It is obvious from the nature of the case that no extension of this kind of explanation to remoter and remoter depths of past time has the slightest tendency to remove this defect.

Before continuing the argument I would point out that nothing that has been said casts any doubt on the theoretical interest or the practical importance of explanation in terms of ordinary causation. When we 'explain' in this way we are learning more and more about the inter-connexions of things and events in time and space. Moreover, by learning these facts, we are enabled to acquire more extensive control over nature, to make new kinds of substances, and to modify the course of future events.

We can now go on with the argument. It is alleged that we can conclude, from the negative facts already stated, that there must be a substance which is neither a part of nature nor nature as a collective whole. And we can conclude that there is another kind of dependence, which is not the ordinary dependence of a later state of affairs on an earlier one in accordance with *de facto* rules of sequence. The existence of this non-natural substance must be intrinsically necessary. And the existence of all natural events and substances must be dependent upon the existence of this non-natural substance by this non-natural kind of dependence.

Let us now consider whether this argument is valid. It may be divided into two parts, negative and positive. Ot the transition from the negative to the positive part there is a suppressed premiss. My criticism will be as follows. (i) I accept the negative part of the argument. (ii) The suppressed premiss, which forms the transition from the negative to the positive part, seems to me to be false.

Therefore I see no reason to accept the conclusion. (iii) I suspect that the conclusion is not only unproven but is either false or meaningless. I will now develop these statements.

(i) What kind of explanations do completely satisfy the human intellect? The human intellect is completely satisfied with a proposition when either (a) the proposition is seen to be intrinsically necessary by direct inspection of its terms, or (b) it is seen to follow by steps, each of which is seen to be intrinsically necessary, from premises which are all seen to be intrinsically necessary. This kind of complete intellectual satisfaction is reached in pure mathematics and hardly anywhere else. Now it is quite certain that no explanation in terms of ordinary causation is capable of giving this kind of satisfaction to the intellect. For no causal law has any trace of self-evidence, and no premiss to the effect that such and such things existed or that such and such events happened in the past has any trace of self-evidence. The causal explanations of science are useful for predicting and controlling the future, for reconstructing the past, and for learning about what is remote in distance or minute in size. But they provide no explanation of anything in the sense in which the proof of a proposition in pure mathematics does provide a completely satisfactory explanation of the mathematical fact asserted by that proposition.

Now it is logically possible that complete intellectual satisfaction should be obtained about natural events and substances if and only if the following conditions were fulfilled. (a) If there were one or more existential propositions which are intrinsically necessary, like mathematical axioms. And (b) if all other true existential propositions followed with strict logical necessity from these, combined, perhaps, with certain intrinsically necessary universal premises. Suppose that these conditions were fulfilled; and suppose, further, that there were a man who *actually knew* these intrinsically necessary premises and *actually saw* in detail that they entail, e.g., the existence at a certain time and place of a person answering to the description of the historical Julius Caesar. Then he would *actually enjoy* complete intellectual satisfaction about the existence of Julius Caesar.

I therefore accept so much as follows of the Cosmological Argument. I admit that no explanation in terms of ordinary causation is capable of giving that kind of intellectual satisfaction about natural things and persons and events which is obtainable about purely mathematical facts. And I admit that, if the universe is such that this kind of intellectual satisfaction is theoretically obtainable about nature, then its structure must be very much as philosophic Theism says that it is.

(ii) The Cosmological Argument claims to prove a categorical proposition, viz. that the universe has this structure. In order to do so it must add a categorical premiss to the hypothetical proposition which I have just admitted. It is plain that this categorical premiss is the proposition that the universe *is* such that this kind of intellectual satisfaction about natural things, persons, and events is, at least in theory, obtainable. This, then, is the suppressed premiss of the argument. Is there any reason to accept it?

We must not unfairly exaggerate what it claims. It is not asserted that any human being ever will in fact enjoy this kind of intellectual satisfaction about nature as a whole or about a single natural thing or person or event. All that is asserted is that the universe is such that a mind, which worked on the same general principles as ours but had indefinitely greater knowledge of detail and power of seeing logical connexions and keeping them before it without confusion, would find every fact about nature perfectly intelligible, in the sense in which everything in pure mathematics is perfectly intelligible to the mathematician. Now I do not see the least reason to believe this. Plainly it is not the kind of premiss for which there is or could be any empirical evidence. Nor is it self-evident or deducible from any premisses which are self-evident. Wherever we have this kind of completely satisfactory insight we are dealing with the formal relations of abstract entities, such as numbers or propositions, and not with the existence or the non-formal properties of particulars. There is no reason whatever to think that this kind of rational insight is possible in the latter case.

(iii) I think that we can go much farther than this in the negative direction. We have seen that an indispensable condition, without which it is logically impossible for nature to be capable of satisfying the intellect in the sense defined, is that there should be some intrinsically necessary existential propositions. Now, in criticizing the Ontological Argument, we saw that 'So-and-so exists' is equivalent to 'There is something which has such and such a set of characteristics', where this set of characteristics constitutes the definition or description of a certain possible object. Therefore an intrinsically necessary existential proposition would be of the form 'There *must be* something which has the characteristics x, y, z, etc.', where this set of characteristics constitutes the definition or description of a certain possible object. Or, to put it the other way round, 'The set of characteristics, x, y, z, etc., *must* together belong to something'.

Now it seems to me evident that there can be no intrinsically necessary propositions of this kind. Necessary propositions are always about the connexion (or disconnexion) of one *attribute* with another *attribute* or one *proposition* with another *proposition,* and they are always *conditional.* They are always of the form 'If anything had the attribute x, it would necessarily have the attribute y', or 'If p were true, then q would be true'. If I am right on this point, it follows that the conclusion of the Cosmological Argument is not only unproven but is false. And it follows that the suppressed premiss of the argument is false. That is, we can be quite certain that the universe cannot be of such a structure that the kind of intellectual satisfaction which is possible in pure mathematics might conceivably be attained about the things and persons and events of nature.

Even if this objection be waived, an equally formidable one remains. Let us suppose, for the sake of argument, that the suppressed premiss is true. Then I think it is easy to show that, even if there were an existent or existents whose existence is intrinsically necessary, this would not in the least help to make nature theoretically intelligible in the sense required. The difficulty is as follows. Anything whose existence was a necessary consequence of its nature would be a *timeless* existent. If a certain set of attributes is such that it *must* belong to something, it is nonsensical to talk of its beginning to belong to something at any date, however far back in the past. It would be like talking of a date at which equilateral triangles began to be equiangular. Now nature is composed of things and persons and processes which begin at certain dates, last for so long, and then cease. But how could a *temporal* fact, such as the fact that there began to be a person having the characteristics of Julius Caesar at a certain date, follow logically from facts all of which are *non-temporal?* Surely it is perfectly obvious that the necessary consequences of facts which are necessary are themselves necessary, and that the necessary consequences of facts which have no reference to any particular time can themselves have no reference to any particular time.

I may therefore sum up my criticisms on the Cosmological Argument as follows. The argument presupposes that nature must be, in principle, capable of satisfying the intellect in the way in which it can be satisfied in pure mathematics. It rightly denies that explanations in terms of ordinary causation, however far back they may be carried, have any tendency to produce this kind of intellectual satisfaction. It argues that such intellectual satisfaction about nature would be in principle obtainable if and only if the two following conditions were fulfilled: (i) that there is at least one particular such that the existence of a particular of that nature is an intrinsically necessary existential fact; (ii) that all facts about the existence of such natural substances as do exist and about the occurrence of such natural events as do occur are necessary consequences of these intrinsically necessary existential facts. The conclusion of the argument is that these two conditions must be fulfilled. Now the objections are these. (i) It is not in the least evident that nature must be in principle capable of satisfying the intellect in this peculiar way. (ii) The first of the two conditions which are necessary for the fulfilment of this demand appears, on reflexion, to be almost devoid of meaning and almost certainly incapable of realization. (iii) Even if the first condition were fulfilled, it is self-evidently impossible that the second should be. For this would require that facts about the existence of things and the occurrence of events at certain dates should be necessary consequences of facts which are all without any temporal reference whatever.

The Divine Circle

Walter T. Stace was born in England in 1886 and was for many years in the British Civil Service in Ceylon. During that time he became a student of Buddhist thought and of idealist philosophy; both had permanent effects upon his thought. In 1932, Stace published The Theory of Knowledge and Existence *in which he defended an idealist position similar to that of Berkeley. In the same year he joined the Department of Philosophy at Princeton and three years later became Stuart Professor there. In recent years he has concentrated on the philosophy of religion and on mysticism both philosophical and religious. His other works include* The Philosophy of Hegel, *1924;* The Concept of Morals, *1937; and* Mysticism and Philosophy, *1960.*

The pure religious consciousness lies in a region which is forever beyond all proof or disproof.

This is a necessary consequence of the "utterly other" character of God from the world, and of the "utterly other" character of the world from God. The eternal order is not the natural order, and the natural order is not the eternal order. The two orders intersect, but in the intersection each remains what it is. Each is wholly self-contained. Therefore it is impossible to pass, by any logical inference, from one to the other. This at once precludes as impossible any talk either of the proof or disproof of religion.

When philosophers and theologians speak of "proofs of the existence of God," or "evidences of Christianity," what they have in mind is always a logical passage from the natural order, or some fact in the natural order, to the divine order. They may, for instance, argue in the following way. Here is the world. That is a natural fact. It must have had a cause. Other natural facts are then pointed out which are supposed to show adaptations of means to ends in nature. Bees pollinate flowers. Surely not by chance, nor following any purpose of their own. Or the heart has the function—which is interpreted as meaning the purpose—of pumping the blood. This teleological mechanism was not made by us, and the purpose evident in it is not our purpose. Therefore the cause of the world must have been an intelligent and designing mind. Doubtless I have much over-simplified the argument, and this version of it might not be accepted by the theologian as a statement of it which is to his liking. Certainly it is not a full statement. That, however, is not the point. The point is that, however the argument is stated, it necessarily starts from the natural order, or from selected facts in the natural order, and ends with a conclusion about the divine reality.

In other cases the natural fact from which the argument starts may be some very astonishing occurrence, which we do not yet know how to explain, and which we therefore call a miracle. This is evidence, it is believed, of a divine intervention.

In all cases we use some fact or facts of the natural order as premises for our argument, and then leap, by an apparently logical inference, clear out of the natural order into the divine order, which thus appears as the conclusion of the argument. The point is that the premise is in the natural world, the conclusion in the divine world.

But an examination of the nature of inference shows that this is an impossible procedure. For inference proceeds always along the thread of some relation. We start with one fact, which is observed. This bears some relation to another fact, which is not observed. We pass along this relation to the second fact. The first fact is our premise, the second fact our conclusion. The relation, in the case of the deductive inference, is that of logical entailment. In non-deductive inferences other relations are used, of which the most common is that of causality. Thus, although the sun is now shining, and the sky is cloudless, I see that the ground is wet, and the trees are dripping with water. I infer that an April shower has passed over, and that it rained a few minutes ago. My inference has passed along the thread of a causal relation from an effect as premise to a cause as conclusion. To pass in this way from facts which are before my eyes, along a relational link, to other facts which are not before my eyes—which are inferred, not seen—is the universal character of inference.

But the natural order is the totality of all things which stand to each other in the one systematic network of relationships which is the universe. Therefore no inference can ever carry me from anything in the natural order to anything outside it. If I start from a natural fact, my inferential process, however long, can end only in another natural fact. A "first cause," simply by virtue of being a cause, would be a fact in the natural order. It is not denied that it might conceivably be possible to argue back from the present state of the world to an intelligent cause of some of its present character- istics—although I do not believe that any such argument is in fact valid. The point is that an intelligent cause of the material world, reached by any such inference, would be only another natural being, a part of the natural order. The point is that such a first cause *would not be God.* It would be at the most a demi-urge. I shall return to this point later.

If God does not lie at the end of any telescope, neither does He lie at the end of any syllogism. I can never, starting from the nat- ural order, prove the divine order. The proof of the divine order must lie, somehow, within itself. It must be its own witness. For it, like the natural order, is complete in itself, self-contained.

But if, for these reasons, God can never be proved by arguments which take natural facts for their premises, for the very same reason He can never be disproved by such arguments. For instance, He cannot be disproved by pointing to the evil and pain in the world.

But if, by arguments of the kind we are considering, the divine order can never be proved, nevertheless God is not without witness. Nor is His being any the less a certainty. But the argument for any- thing within the divine order must start from within the divine order. The divine order, however, is not far off. It is not beyond the stars. It is within us—as also within all other things. God exists in the eternal moment which is in every man, either self-consciously present and fully revealed, or buried, more or less deeply, in the unconscious. We express this in poetic language if we say that God is "in the heart." It is in the heart, then, that the witness of Him, the proof of Him, must lie, and not in any external circumstance of the natural order. So far as theology is concerned, we had better leave the bees and their pollination of flowers alone.

That the divine cannot be made the subject of proof is merely another aspect of the truth that the mystical illumination is inca- pable of conceptualization. For this means that God is inaccessible to the logical intellect. The attempt to prove His existence is an attempt to reach Him through concepts, and is therefore fore- doomed to failure. The doctrine of the negative divine implies the same conclusion. For its meaning is that the door to an understand- ing of God is barred against the concept, and therefore against logical argument. And all this comes to the same as saying that God is known only by intuition, not by the logical intellect.

Every religious proposition, not only that which asserts the existence of God, is derived from religious intuition, and is incapable of any other proof. This is true not only of all the creeds of all the great religions. It is true of all religious statements made anywhere—of the propositions, for instance, contained in this book. Either they are based on intuitions, or they are baseless. Neither can they be, by the reader, submitted to the test of any logical proof or disproof. Their appeal is in the end solely to the reader's own religious intuition.

It is easy to be mistaken about this. The reader may, of course, argue. He may say, for instance, "such and such a proposition, which is asserted in this book, agrees, or does not agree, with the Catholic faith; and therefore it is true, or false." And the Catholic theologians themselves argued, and continue to argue. But the Catholic faith itself is ultimately based on nothing else but intuition. Thus in any theological argument the ultimate premise must be an intuition. From that point on the argument will proceed by logical steps to its conclusion. But the intuition itself is incapable of being proved by any argument. This is more conventionally expressed by saying that theology is based on revelation, and that all theological reasoning takes place within the framework of revealed truth. For revelation and intuition are two words for the same thing. In this book, as in other theological writings, there are, of course, trains of reasoning. But they remain always within the circle of ideas whose ultimate basis is intuitive. Their purpose is to show that one such idea is consistent with another, or that a suggested idea is inconsistent with some other proposition already intuitively accepted. They never argue from the outside, that is, from the natural order, to the divine order.

It may be discovered that one proposition of the theological system contradicts another. This will be due to one of two causes. Either the contradiction is ultimate and irremediable, as in the doctrine of the Trinity—a condition which will be discussed in the next chapter—or, in the case of merely subordinate propositions, it will show that there has been some mistake in the interpretation of the intuitions at the base of the system. But if the system is internally self-consistent, then as a whole it stands or falls solely on the basis of its intuitive appeal. If it is taken as a whole, as a completed circle of ideas, there is no way in which it can be supported or attacked from the outside. A system of religious beliefs is a symbolic account of the divine order. Outside of the divine order there is nothing except the natural order. Therefore to say that the circle of ideas, which are thus symbolically expository of the divine order, cannot be supported or attacked from the outside, is the same as saying that no proof or disproof of them which takes as its premises facts within the natural order is possible.

Those beliefs about God, about eternity, about the divine order, about the ultimate divine nature of the world, which constitute the body of what we call religious beliefs, and which we have attempted to elucidate in the preceding chapters, possess in this way the character of circularity. Each of them may logically imply the others, but none of them, nor all of them taken together, are implied by anything outside their own circle. They constitute the divine circle. No doubt in our treatment of the divine circle in this book we have failed in sundry ways to exhibit the mutual implication of religious truths. There will be found in it inconsistencies, incoherences, dark places, obscurities. This will be the fault of our treatment, not of the truths themselves. The point to be seized is that, whether we have succeeded or failed in our exposition, all religious reasoning must, if it is truly understood, be circular. And this means that nothing in the divine order is ever either implied or contradicted by anything in the natural order; and that religious truth in general can never be either proved or disproved.

We must bear in mind that we are speaking here not of religion itself but of religious beliefs, that is to say, of those propositions by means of which the intellect seeks to interpret symbolically to itself that inner and ultimate experience which is religion itself. We may imagine the religious experience as a sun, below which, and depending from which, hangs the circle of religious ideas or propositions. It is unsupported from below, from the earth, that is, from the natural order. And it is these propositions which, we say, cannot be derived by deduction or induction from anything within the natural order. They are to be derived only from the religious experience. To say of religion itself that it cannot be deductively or inductively derived would be meaningless. For religion is the experience, not the beliefs. And it has no meaning to speak of deducing or proving an experience. It is only propositions which are the subject matter of proof, demonstration, argument.

A. J. AYER

The Critique of Theology

Alfred J. Ayer was born in 1910 and was first a student and then a Lecturer in Philosophy at Christ Church, Oxford. He has held the Grote Professorship at the University of London and is presently the Wykeham Professor of Logic in Oxford University. Ayer is best known for his book Language, Truth and Logic, *which still remains the classic text of logical positivism in the Anglo-American form. Adopting the view that a sentence is meaningful only if it is verifiable in sense experience, Ayer sought to eliminate metaphysics and theology and at the same time reduce ethics to subjective feeling. Ayer's thought has continued to develop, as is clear from his most recent book,* The Concept of a Person (1963). *His other works are* The Foundations of Empirical Knowledge (1940), Thinking and Meaning (1947), The Problem of Knowledge (1956), *and* Philosophical Essays (1954).

It is now generally admitted, at any rate by philosophers, that the existence of a being having the attributes which define the god of any non-animistic religion cannot be demonstratively proved. To see that this is so, we have only to ask ourselves what are the premises from which the existence of such a god could be deduced. If the conclusion that a god exists is to be demonstratively certain, then these premises must be certain; for, as the conclusion of a deductive argument is already contained in the premises, any uncertainty there may be about the truth of the premises is necessarily shared by it. But we know that no empirical proposition can ever be anything more than probable. It is only *a priori* propositions that are logically certain. But we cannot deduce the existence of a god from an *a priori* proposition. For we know that the reason why *a priori* propositions are certain is that they are tautologies. And from a set of tautologies nothing but a further tautology can be validly deduced. It follows that there is no possibility of demonstrating the existence of a god.

What is not so generally recognised is that there can be no way of proving that the existence of a god, such as the God of Christianity, is even probable. Yet this also is easily shown. For if the

From A. J. Ayer, *Language, Truth and Logic* (2d ed.; London: Victor Gollancz, Ltd, 1946), pp. 114–117. Used by permission of the author.

54

existence of such a god were probable, then the proposition that he existed would be an empirical hypothesis. And in that case it would be possible to deduce from it, and other empirical hypotheses, certain experiential propositions which were not deducible from those other hypotheses alone. But in fact this is not possible. It is sometimes claimed, indeed, that the existence of a certain sort of regularity in nature constitutes sufficient evidence for the existence of a god. But if the sentence "God exists" entails no more than that certain types of phenomena occur in certain sequences, then to assert the existence of a god will be simply equivalent to asserting that there is the requisite regularity in nature; and no religious man would admit that this was all he intended to assert in asserting the existence of a god. He would say that in talking about God, he was talking about a transcendent being who might be known through certain empirical manifestations, but certainly could not be defined in terms of those manifestations. But in that case the term "god" is a metaphysical term. And if "god" is a metaphysical term, then it cannot be even probable that a god exists. For to say that "God exists" is to make a metaphysical utterance which cannot be either true or false. And by the same criterion, no sentence which purports to describe the nature of a transcendent god can possess any literal significance.

It is important not to confuse this view of religious assertions with the view that is adopted by atheists, or agnostics.[1] For it is characteristic of an agnostic to hold that the existence of a god is a possibility in which there is no good reason either to believe or disbelieve; and it is characteristic of an atheist to hold that it is at least probable that no god exists. And our view that all utterances about the nature of God are nonsensical, so far from being identical with, or even lending any support to, either of these familiar contentions, is actually incompatible with them. For if the assertion that there is a god is nonsensical, then the atheist's assertion that there is no god is equally nonsensical, since it is only a significant proposition that can be significantly contradicted. As for the agnostic, although he refrains from saying either that there is or that there is not a god, he does not deny that the question whether a transcendent god exists is a genuine question. He does not deny that the two sentences "There is a transcendent god" and "There is no transcendent god" express propositions one of which is actually true and the

---

[1] This point was suggested to me by Professor H. H. Price.

other false. All he says is that we have no means of telling which of them is true, and therefore ought not to commit ourselves to either. But we have seen that the sentences in question do not express propositions at all. And this means that agnosticism also is ruled out.

Thus we offer the theist the same comfort as we gave to the moralist. His assertions cannot possibly be valid, but they cannot be invalid either. As he says nothing at all about the world, he cannot justly be accused of saying anything false, or anything for which he has insufficient grounds. It is only when the theist claims that in asserting the existence of a transcendent god he is expressing a genuine proposition that we are entitled to disagree with him.

It is to be remarked that in cases where deities are identified with natural objects, assertions concerning them may be allowed to be significant. If, for example, a man tells me that the occurrence of thunder is alone both necessary and sufficient to establish the truth of the proposition that Jehovah is angry, I may conclude that, in his usage of words, the sentence "Jehovah is angry" is equivalent to "It is thundering." But in sophisticated religions, though they may be to some extent based on men's awe of natural process which they cannot sufficiently understand, the "person" who is supposed to control the empirical world is not himself located in it; he is held to be superior to the empirical world, and so outside it; and he is endowed with super-empirical attributes. But the notion of a person whose essential attributes are non-empirical is not an intelligible notion at all. We may have a word which is used as if it named this "person," but, unless the sentences in which it occurs express propositions which are empirically verifiable, it cannot be said to symbolize anything. And this is the case with regard to the word "god," in the usage in which it is intended to refer to a transcendent object. The mere existence of the noun is enough to foster the illusion that there is a real, or at any rate a possible entity corresponding to it. It is only when we enquire what God's attributes are that we discover that "God," in this usage, is not a genuine name.

It is common to find belief in a transcendent god conjoined with belief in an after-life. But, in the form which it usually takes, the content of this belief is not a genuine hypothesis. To say that men do not ever die, or that the state of death is merely a state of prolonged insensibility, is indeed to express a significant proposition, though all the available evidence goes to show that it is false. But to say that there is something imperceptible inside a man, which is his soul or his real self, and that it goes on living after he is dead, is to make a metaphysical assertion which has no more factual content than the assertion that there is a transcendent god.

It is worth mentioning that, according to the account which we have given of religious assertions, there is no logical ground for antagonism between religion and natural science. As far as the question of truth or falsehood is concerned, there is no opposition between the natural scientist and the theist who believes in a transcendent god. For since the religious utterances of the theist are not genuine propositions at all, they cannot stand in any logical relation to the propositions of science. Such antagonism as there is between religion and science appears to consist in the fact that science takes away one of the motives which make men religious. For it is acknowledged that one of the ultimate sources of religious feeling lies in the inability of men to determine their own destiny; and science tends to destroy the feeling of awe with which men regard an alien world, by making them believe that they can understand and anticipate the course of natural phenomena, and even to some extent control it. The fact that it has recently become fashionable for physicists themselves to be sympathetic towards religion is a point in favour of this hypothesis. For this sympathy towards religion marks the physicists' own lack of confidence in the validity of their hypotheses, which is a reaction on their part from the antireligious dogmatism of nineteenth-century scientists, and a natural outcome of the crisis through which physics has just passed.

PART II
God and Nature

A . B O Y C E   G I B S O N

The Two Ideas of God

Alexander Boyce Gibson was born in 1900 and spent the early days of his teaching career as Lecturer in Philosophy at Birmingham University. In 1935 he accepted an appointment at the University of Melbourne in Australia where he is currently Professor of Philosophy. Boyce Gibson has long been interested in the philosophy of religion and in the mutual relevance of metaphysical and theological topics. His works include Christianity, Democracy and Dictatorship (1940), The Philosophy of Descartes (1932), *and* Thinkers at Work (*with A. A. Phillips*) (1946).

Throughout the history of Western philosophy there have been two competing conceptions of divinity, which will be called the self-sufficient and the outgoing. The object of this paper is to see if it is possible to maintain both conceptions at the same time, and, if so, on what conditions. The issue appears to be of the first importance to natural theology, because it would be permanently impoverished if either conception were dropped and yet there is a *prima facie* contradiction between them.

On the one hand, in the Western tradition, God is said to be complete in Himself, and does not require to be supplemented by His creation. He moves the world, as Aristotle said, "by being loved," and not by any active manifestations on His own part; for that would indicate that He was previously inadequate. He is eternal and unchangeable, unaffected by anything that can happen, within or without Himself. It would make no difference to Him if the creatures did not exist at all. He does not suffer with their sufferings: even in the Christian orbit, to suppose that He does is to admit to the heresy—my favorite heresy—of Patripassionism. He is ineffable, motionless and utterly alone.

On the other hand, in the Western tradition, God is a creator: He brings into being what was not; "we love Him because He first loved us"; He intervenes in the world and faces towards the world; He is accessible to prayer; it is a matter of concern to Him that the

Reprinted from A. Boyce Gibson, "The Two Strands in Natural Theology," *The Monist*, Vol. XLVII, No. 3 (1963), pp. 335–353, by permission of the Open Court Publishing Co., La Salle, Ill.

world should be as good as it can be; and on one famous occasion He worked six full days in the week. And (lest it be thought that we are drifting too far from nature to revelation) Thomas Aquinas, speaking as a philosopher, exulted in the variety of things: "the diversity of creatures was primarily intended by the prime agent": and he was followed in this by the heretical Giordano Bruno; "the gods take pleasure in the multiform representation of multiple things"; though Bruno was indiscreet or indifferent enough to write "gods" in the plural. And, finally, there was Leibniz, who attached the creatures to the creator by the iron chain of sufficient reason.

Now these two aspects of the Western tradition are *prima facie* opposed to each other. How can the immobile move anything? How can the unchangeable have purposes? How can the eternal deploy itself in time? How can creatures be at once of no account and of high concern? If, as would appear, we are confronted with contradictions, is it then possible to adjust them so that they are contradictions no longer? Or, alternatively, is it possible that one or the other is a mistake, and that the tradition henceforward should run on one engine rather than on two? One thing is certain: that until these problems are faced, natural theology is living in (let us say) a natural's paradise.

It is customary with theologians to say that these two persisting tendencies are Greek and Hebrew respectively. Whether the second or outgoing side of the tradition exhausts the Hebrew contribution experts must judge; but the fashionable theologians' view about the Greeks is certainly a mistake. The doubleness (some might say duplicity) of the Western theological tradition existed already in Greek philosophy, and especially in Plato. Over against the mysticism of the *Symposium* and the sixth book of the *Republic* we must set the creationism of the *Timaeus* and the tenth Book of the *Laws*. We must also add that in the formation of the Western tradition in the Middle Ages the *Timaeus* counted for more than all the other dialogues put together. . . .

We can now examine the two strands in Western natural theology in greater detail.

The first, which we shall call the "immobilist," we shall illustrate by referring to the second book of Plato's *Republic*, which contains a frontal and revolutionary attack on the popular religion of Ancient Greece. The myths, whether poetic or obscene, purported to show forth the divine by metamorphosis; thus God is known as such by

His magical power of becoming something else. Plato's response to popular religion was that while it might be good enough for gods it was not good enough for his commonwealth; and he set about re-forming the gods by turning them into highlights of the rationalist state—a process finally completed only in *Laws X*. His first step was to insist that what is divine (singular or plural), being perfect, cannot change; for if what is perfect changes, it will not be as perfect as before (381b). This applies particularly if the change comes from outside, for that would mean that God is being pushed about by extraneous forces; but applies also to voluntary change (one thinks of Zeus becoming a bull to abduct Europa), and even to the simulation of change by the actually changeless, for simula-tion is a form of lying appropriate (I use Plato's language) not to gods but to poets. Changelessness, then, is the central character of deity; and one can see in this conviction both the indignation of a religious reformer and an expression of the philosophy of Forms.

But if the gods are changeless there must be a world of change which is intercepted and left outside the divine perfection. Other-wise there would be no point in the contrast: in a homogeneously changeless world no one would call *anything* changeless. Further, that world is not *because* of divine perfection, but in spite of it: it may aspire after it; when self-conscious it may discipline itself to attain to it; and in a few cases it may actually succeed. But in those cases the mortal is "translated," and the rest of mortality re-mains behind him. It is thus entailed in the notion of a changeless God that that which changes is outside his province. He is out there, beyond, an eternal lure to both mind and heart, but totally unresponsive—how could He respond, seeing that to respond is to change? So it is thus further entailed that the cosmos is a dualism with the gods and the Forms on one side and all changing things on the other. This conclusion is in conflict with much else in the Western theological tradition, but it is certainly what happens if the changeless is taken neat. What has made it palatable is being diluted with its opposite.

Further, that which is changeless is self-sufficient. Indeed, for the Greeks, it might be more accurate to say that that which is self-sufficient is changeless; αυταρκεια, self-sufficiency, was the more fa-miliar conception; it was the watchword of city-state economics. But, either way, the entailment holds. What is changeless has need of nothing, and what has need of nothing has no need to change.

What the idea of self-sufficiency in theology amounts to (again, when taken neat) may be gauged from a revealing passage of the *Eudemian Ethics,* which, if not Aristotle, is so near to the source that it hardly matters: "The self-sufficient man neither needs useful people nor people to cheer him, nor society; his own society is enough for him. This is most plain in the case of a god; for it is clear that, needing nothing, he will not need a friend, nor have one." [1]

To the activist strand we now turn: and the best introduction to it is through the philosophical difficulties of the alternative.

As long as the mind is on the upward path, receding from the temporal scene to the unimaginable heights of reason, it does not have to face the question, How and why does the temporal scene exist at all? The temporal scene is the starting point of the dialectic in which it is to be transcended. But, from the point of view of the changeless, the temporal scene is strictly superfluous. And yet it is not nothing. In the *Republic* Plato declared it both being and not-being, and used the metaphors of participation and imitation to explain its relation to being. But this is no more than an honest statement of the problem. The temporal scene has being, in a sort of a way, but there is nothing in the nature of being to suggest why. The same problem will always arise when the standpoint of the ascent is taken as final. Even when it is trying to surpass itself, the finite can never be final. There is just *no* reason why the temporal scene should have the being it does have: if it is there, it bears testimony to something in the world other than reason, with which reason is only just on speaking terms. This is where there creeps into the picture the dualism which the centralizing force of the good should have dissipated. But as long as no reason is given for the temporal scene being what it is and is admitted to be, the dualism must persist. . . .

It is time now to turn to the second or outgoing strand of our theological tradition.

The central conception here is that of creation. Now a creator

---

[1] *Eudemian Ethics,* trans. Solomon, Oxford translations, 9, 6, 1244 b6. I have replaced the translator's "independent" by "self-sufficient," the usual translation of ἀυταρκής.

At this point tradition would insist on a discussion of the further attribute of necessity. It is true that the changeless and self-sufficient God is also claimed to be necessary; but God might still be claimed to be necessary without being timeless or self-sufficient.

differs from a demiurge in having no pre-existing models or materials. Everything that is, He has made. There is therefore no difficulty about dualism; if there is a difficulty, it is that there appears to be no room for the minimum of dualism which most people hanker after. There is also a sure foundation, as there is not under immobilism, for the uniformity of nature.[2] Again, there is a natural alignment, at least in the West, between this kind of theology and personal religion. An immobile God is inaccessible: to pray to Him is merely to commune devoutly with one's own thoughts. The God who moves can also be moved. And here difficulties arise, for a god who can be moved is no longer self-sufficient; he has "passions," which even the accommodating Thirty-Nine Articles declare He has not; and He moves on from one point to the next, which is inconciliable with the Greek dogma of timelessness. Indeed, the moment we talk of creation, the whole problem of time arises to plague us. For either creation is in time or it is not; if it is not, it differs hardly, if at all from emanation, which is hardly, if at all, activity; if it is, the usual barrage of questions about what happens before creation is strictly in order, and if anything happens before creation, time is not a creation but part of God's nature.

These are not historical accidents; they are implicit in the original concept. Activity is necessarily in time, even in the form of creation. Only a stationary God can be eternal. The practical difference to the believer may be slight; for him "from everlasting to everlasting" is as good as "eternal"; in fact he does not distinguish between them. But for the creationist philosopher "from everlasting to everlasting" is opposed to "eternal," and is the only logically acceptable formula. (It is the believer's best formula anyhow, for it is far more biblical.) For to create, in even the most attenuated sense, is to be the reason why something is which formerly was not; and the operative word is "formerly." The state of affairs before the thing happened *differs* from the state of affairs afterwards. It is just not possible to say that creating makes no difference to the creator, for the something which is there, and formerly was not there, is in relation to Him: He is related where formerly He was unrelated.

Thus the second strand in natural theology, left to itself, arrives at conclusions which are in contradiction with the first strand, left to itself. . . .

[2] This point was admirably made by Collingwood in his *Essay on Metaphysics,* p. 253.

But, leaving for a moment the history of the matter, let us consider on what terms, if at all, the synthesis of the two conceptions of Godhead could have been effected.

(1) It would have been easy to keep the Greek categories for the intellectuals and to dispense the primitive Christian categories as mythology for the multitude: easy, because both would thus have followed their natural bent. In fact, and fortunately, this did not happen: what that way leads to can be seen in the intellectual sterilization of Islam after Averroes, who, *mutatis mutandis*, made precisely this distinction. Both categories persisted (though with differing emphasis) both in natural theology *and* in the creeds to which all subscribed. The category of activity was not consigned to revelation and discarded from philosophy. The philosophical problem, on the contrary, was fairly faced on both levels.

(2) In revealed theology, it was all too convenient to assign the diverse attributes to different persons of the Trinity. In general, the God of the Old Testament was provided with Aristotelean attributes, and activity of Godhead was assigned to the Son.[3] This nest of confusions is strictly beyond the scope of this paper; we may simply quote "I and the Father are one," "He that hath seen me hath seen the Father," and above all, "My Father *worketh hitherto,* and I work." It is mentioned because it provides an allegedly Christian escape from our dilemma: the divergent attributes can be assigned to the different Persons. Unfortunately,[4] it is the first Person of the Trinity which appears in Aristotelean garb, and it is the first Person of the Trinity that is discussed in natural, as opposed to revealed, theology. Hence the revealed dissociation of Persons helps to maintain, for the philosophers, the immobilist conception of God.

(3) Thus there is no way round: we have to accept both the Aristotelean and the Hebrew inheritance, and let them sort themselves out as best as they can. How, then, starting with immobilism, eternity, and self-sufficiency, can we derive the attributes of creativity, justice and mercy?

(a) One device is to say that we just can't, and can't be expected to: so great a mystery can't be explained at all, it has to be accepted, humbly and empirically, as a fact. Such an attribute is fair enough at the moment of worship, when analysis is suspended; but it is im-

---

[3] As Collingwood points out, *Essay in Metaphysics*, p. 226.

[4] As well as unnaturally: The God of the Old Testament is particularly non-Aristotelean.

)roper in natural theology, which is committed to getting the analysis straight.

(b) Another device is to develop the notion of self-sufficiency so as to *include* the notion of outgoingness. Its merit is that it maintains the note of one-sided dependence which is undoubtedly part of religion and which the notion of self-sufficiency conveys, but not quite so well. A self-sufficient God may easily encourage self-sufficiency in men; in fact, the "divine" man, i.e., the sage, is a sort of prefiguration of Him. An outgoing God, by His generosity, elicits both generosity in others and gratitude to Himself. The passage from self-sufficiency to outgoingness has thus been made acceptable to Western religion; and it has the advantage of requiring the co-operation of no other force outside God Himself. "Outgoing" is a metaphor designed to express what happens when the abundance of God can no longer be contained in God and has to spill over into creation. Unhappily, the notion of self-sufficiency does not cohere with that of abundance, but excludes it. For (1) what is self-sufficient cannot add to its inward resources any more than it can be lacking in them. (2) Only through an addition to the inward resources of God could there be an overflow. (3) And principally, both operations postulate a passage of time for the self-sufficient timeless God to deploy Himself in. Time is thus installed in the centre of the divine being, and the "eternal" is overthrown. To develop self-sufficiency by means of "overflowing" is therefore suicidal and if "overflowing" is acceptable, for religious or philosophical reasons, self-sufficiency will have to go.

(c) Yet another attempt to combine the incompatible is to be found in the conception of God's goodness. Aristotle himself presents God as good; and the general notion that what is one and what is good are somehow the same is a leading motif of Greek psychology and politics. Now the oneness and the goodness of God was precisely what had to be stressed by early Christian theologians in their struggle with pagan polytheism and the Manichees. Here, if anywhere it might be said, there should be continuity.

On the oneness of God we may agree: on this issue Aristotle was with his Christian adapters against the Greek tradition. But the senses in which "goodness" was understood in the two environments were so different that the bridge proves to be no more than verbal. In Aristotle the "good" is that to which everything tends; God is good as the finally satisfying object of the world's desire. To be good in this sense does not entail *doing* anything. But the goodness of God in the Old and New Testaments is displayed in His justice and His mercy: and these are unquestionably thought of as activities. They are, moreover, activities which no self-sufficient deity, enthroned above time, could possibly engage in; for Him, they would be a descent: "omnis determinatio est negatio," as Spinoza was to say later on. Nor is it any use saying that on the Christian view there *was* a descent; *if* there was, it was because God was in some way pledged to this world, i.e., He is not self-sufficient.

(d) Nothing has been said about the attribute of "necessity" so commonly taken to distinguish the being of God from other kinds of being: partly because everything cannot be said at once, but mainly because "necessary being" might be shown not to be inseparable from self-sufficiency and timelessness, and these are the attributes under scrutiny. It might, in fact, be possible to transpose the arguments for necessary being into the temporal mode. This will be argued in the next paragraph. All that is here said is that self-sufficiency and timelessness must stand on their own feet; and this we have now seen they have some difficulty in doing.

W . T . S T A C E

The Two World Pictures

In the modern epoch the two world-pictures, that which I have called the naturalistic or scientific view of the world and that which I have called the religious view, face one another in unresolved contradiction. I have said that modern culture has for its essence the conflict between them. It is not to be solved by amiable "reconciliations" between bishops and scientists. The notion that it has been settled because ecclesiastics now agree that the question of the age of the earth, of whether the heliocentric or the geocentric astronomy is true, of whether man is a "special creation" or is descended from simian ancestors, belong to the province of science and not to that of religion, is a sheer delusion. For science, as we have tried to show, is irrelevant to the problem. The problem is handed over to the philosophers because it is a matter of general world-views, and not of the details of any science. Moreover, any mere compromise, by which one part of the territory of the world is given to science, the other part to religion, is worthless and shallow. This was the great insight of Kant and of the romantic movement of the nineteenth century—whatever may be thought of the particular solutions offered by Kant and the romantics. Thus the problem still stands before us, unsolved by any rapprochements which have occurred, or are likely to occur, between scientists and religious men.

The question may perhaps be put in the form: is religion, or is anything in any religion, true? For it can hardly be the case that the religious view of the world in general is true, but that all particular religions are wholly false. And if the question be put in this form—is any religion true?—I should myself, until recently, have replied with an unqualified no. Religion, I should have said, is nothing but a mass of false ideas and superstitions of which the ultimate source is wishful thinking. We have believed a view of the world which we want to believe, namely, that is ruled by a power which is friendly to us and to the values of beauty and goodness which we cherish. As a result of further study and reflection I have modified this opinion. To the question asked I now find the answer to be a qualified yes.

To explain this is the object of the present chapter. I fear that its contents must appear, in a peculiar sense, no more than the very personal opinions of a single man. I offer them for what they are worth.

It will be helpful to begin by regarding the religious view of the world, not as a set of intellectual propositions about the nature of the world, but as importing a way of life. Of course any religion is, or implies, some complex of propositions about the universe. But every religion offers a way of life. And I shall consider religion in this aspect first, leaving its intellectual side, as a set of beliefs about the world, for consideration later in this chapter.

I will quote three passages from T. S. Eliot's play *The Cocktail Party*.[1] They come from different parts of the play, but it is noteworthy that they are all three put into the mouth of the same character, whose utterances, in some sense, carry the main message of the drama. Whatever else there is in the play, it certainly teaches that there are two possible ways of life between which we have to make a choice. Says the character Reilly concerning human life:

> The best of a bad job is all that any of us make of it—
> *Except, of course, the saints.*

In a later context he says:

> There *is* another way, if you have the courage.
> The first I could describe in familiar terms
> Because you have seen it, as we all have seen it,
> Illustrated, more or less, in the lives of those
>   about us.
> The second is *unknown*, and so requires faith—
> The kind of faith that issues from despair.
> *The destination cannot be described;*
> *You will know very little until you get there;*
> You will journey blind. But the way leads
>   towards possession
> Of what you have sought for in the wrong
>   place.

[1] T. S. Eliot, *The Cocktail Party*. Quoted by permission of the publishers, Harcourt, Brace and Company, Inc. The italics in these quotations are all mine except the word "is" in the first line of the second quotation which is Mr. Eliot's.

In the third passage, quoted from a later page, Reilly says:

> But such *experience* can only be hinted at
> In *myths and images*. To speak about it
> We talk of darkness, labyrinths, Minotaur ter-
> rors.

There is then a "way," and an "experience," and a "destination." It is the way of the "saints." Nevertheless it is "unknown." Also it is only for those who "have the courage." The destination "cannot be described." The experience likewise cannot be described, but is only "hinted at in myths and images." I shall suggest that these words, a "way" or path, followed by the "saints," which leads to an "experience" and a "destination" which "cannot be known" except through "myths and images," stand for the conceptions which are the essential truth of all religions.

In every religion there is a way or a path, and there is a destination or experience to which it leads. "I am the way, the truth and the life," says the Jesus of St. John's gospel. The Buddhist speaks of "the noble eightfold path." The destination, the experience—which is hidden—is variously described as "salvation," "heaven," "nirvana," "union with Brahman." The different religions seem to refer to different paths and different destinations. I shall maintain that always and everywhere, in all the great religions, there is in fact only one destination, one experience, even—with some qualification—one path, but that it is "hinted at" by means of different "myths and images" which constitute the differences between the religions.

Mr. Eliot gives to his own words, if I understand him, a specially Christian interpretation. Thus the end of the play seems to teach that the "way" necessarily, or at least usually, leads through martyrdom which, if taken in its literal sense of death for the faith, is a peculiarly Christian conception. (All religions, of course, involve martyrdom, if by that is meant only the destruction in us of the desires of the world.) I do not know whether in this I interpret Mr. Eliot rightly. But in any case I shall not follow him in any specifically Christian interpretation he may give to his own words. I have made it clear before that in my view religion and the religious view of the world are not the special property of Christian peoples, but belong to the universal heritage of mankind. It does not matter whether the meanings which I shall give to Mr. Eliot's words are his meanings or not. I shall use them to express my own meanings. I shall give them a more universal scope than he perhaps intends. What he says, apparently only of one religion, applies, I shall contend, to all the great religions.

The myths and images by means of which we hint at the experience and the destination are, in my view, though perhaps not in Mr. Eliot's, the creeds and dogmas of the different religions. These vary and contradict one another, and herein lie the differences between the religions. The unity between them lies, in the first instance, in the path and the destination, the way of life, which is the way of the saints. By the word "saint" perhaps Mr. Eliot means to refer only to the Christian saints. But I shall mean the saints of any religion. Whether this way implies any common view of the nature of the world is something which I shall discuss later in this chapter. Thus there are three questions which we have to discuss:

(1) The conception of religious dogmas and doctrines as myths and images.
(2) The way of life, the destination, the experience.
(3) Whether the experience implies any special view of the nature of the universe.

That all religious doctrines and dogmas are myths and images means that none of them is *literally* true. To have perceived this is the contribution made to thought by the skeptics and the atheists, in fact by the scientific view of the world. But they have missed something. They have simply said that the dogmas are not true. In this they were right. What they failed to see was that the dogmas are not merely falsehoods, but that they are myths, images, allegories which hint at a way of life, a destination, an experience, and possibly also—this is the question referred to in (3) above, which is left for later discussion—some deeper truth about the universe. What we have first to show is that the dogmas are, if understood literally, false. Hence the contentions of the next few pages, which will be designed to show this, will seem like pure atheism and skepticism. But they must be understood in the light of the later parts of this chapter.

Naturally I cannot take all the dogmas of all the great religions and show that, if taken literally, they are false. Such a task would be almost endless. Nor is it at all necessary. Practically all religious people hold that the doctrines which are special and peculiar to religions other than their own are false. The Christian does not accept the Hindu doctrine of reincarnation. The Buddhist does not accept the Christian doctrine of the Trinity. The procedure I shall adopt will be to take only one dogma, which is common to most religions, and which will be thought by most people to be *the* most fundamental doctrine of religion, and show that, if it is understood literally, there is no reason to believe that it is true, and every reason to suppose that it is false. This is the doctrine that there exists a being, known as God, who is a person, a mind, a consciousness, who formed a plan in his mind, and who, in accordance with his purpose, created a world. I do not think that this can be "proved" to be false. It is conceivable that there might be such a mind who made the world as a watchmaker makes a watch. But I think it can be shown that there is no reason at all to think that there is such a being, and that the conception of him in fact involves such difficulties that we are compelled to give it up. That the doctrine of God may have a symbolic meaning, which is true, is something the discussion of which is postponed to a later page. It is only the literal meaning of it with which we are now concerned.

The first thing to say is that science has absolutely nothing to do with the matter. This should be obvious from what has already been said in earlier chapters. It does not make any difference to the doctrine of the existence of God whether the sun goes round the earth or the earth round the sun, whether the planets move in circles or ellipses, whether the laws of motion are what Galileo and Newton thought or not. The transition from the teachings of early science to a diminishing belief in God was a psychological, not a logical transition. In other words, it was a mistake. It is true that the scientific belief that all events are wholly to be explained by natural causes, and that there are no supernatural interventions, does make real difficulties for the more primitive and naïve ideas of God's action in the world. But even this, as was shown previously, can be overcome by a little logical ingenuity. We have only to suppose that God's existence is necessary to the continued existence of the world, and that he acts in it, now as in the past, always through and by means of, the operation of natural laws. And if Newtonian science contained nothing inconsistent with belief in God, neither does the science of today. No science ever could.

The kind of thought which is really fatal to literal belief in religious dogmas has always come from philosophers, not from scientists. The popular belief to the contrary, which is a delusion, is partly due to the mistaken transitions of thought already referred to, and partly to the fact that science is in everybody's mouth (the modern idol), while philosophy is unknown except to a few people.

ALFRED NORTH WHITEHEAD

God and the World

Alfred North Whitehead was born in England in 1861. After a distinguished career at Cambridge and London, he came to America in 1924 where he became Professor of Philosophy at Harvard University. The work of Whitehead has been of central importance in the philosophy of the twentieth century. Few philosophers have been able to combine as he did technical skill in logic and mathematics with a speculative vision of reality as a whole. Whitehead's "process" philosophy represents one of the original synoptic philosophies of recent decades. A mathematician and collaborator with Bertrand Russell in the production of Principia Mathematica (*3 vols., 1910–1913*), *Whitehead wrote extensively about science, religion, education, and civilization. Among his many books are* The Principles of Natural Knowledge (*1919*), The Concept of Nature (*1920*), Science and the Modern World (*1925*), and* Adventures of Ideas (*1933*). He died in 1947.

There is another side to the nature of God which cannot be omitted. Throughout this exposition of the philosophy of organism we have been considering the primary action of God on the world. From this point of view, he is the principle of concretion—the principle whereby there is initiated a definite outcome from a situation otherwise riddled with ambiguity. Thus, so far, the primordial side of the nature of God has alone been relevant.

But God, as well as being primordial, is also consequent. He is the beginning and the end. He is not the beginning in the sense of being in the past of all members. He is the presupposed actuality of conceptual operation, in unison of becoming with every other creative act. Thus by reason of the relativity of all things, there is a reaction of the world on God. The completion of God's nature into a fulness of physical feeling is derived from the objectification of the world in God. He shares with every new creation its actual world; and the concrescent creature is objectified in God as a novel element in God's objectification of that actual world. This prehension into God of each creature is directed with the subjective aim, and clothed with the subjective form, wholly derivative from his all-inclusive primordial valuation. God's conceptual nature is unchanged, by reason of its final completeness. But his derivative nature is consequent upon the creative advance of the world.

Thus, analogously to all actual entities, the nature of God is dipolar. He has a primordial nature and a consequent nature. The consequent nature of God is conscious; and it is the realization of the actual world in the unity of his nature, and through the transformation of his wisdom. The primordial nature is conceptual, the consequent nature is the weaving of God's physical feelings upon his primordial concepts.

One side of God's nature is constituted by his conceptual experience. This experience is the primordial fact in the world, limited by no actuality which it presupposes. It is therefore infinite, devoid of all negative prehensions. This side of his nature is free, complete, primordial, eternal, actually deficient, and unconscious. The other side originates with physical experience derived from the temporal world, and then acquires integration with the primordial side. It is determined, incomplete, consequent, 'everlasting,' fully actual, and conscious. His necessary goodness expresses the determination of his consequent nature.

Conceptual experience can be infinite, but it belongs to the nature of physical experience that it is finite. An actual entity in the temporal world is to be conceived as originated by physical experience with its process of completion motivated by consequent, conceptual experience initially derived from God. God is to be conceived as originated by conceptual experience with his process of completion motivated by consequent, physical experience, initially derived from the temporal world.

The perfection of God's subjective aim, derived from the completeness of his primordial nature, issues into the character of his consequent nature. In it there is no loss, no obstruction. The world is felt in a unison of immediacy. The property of combining creative advance with the retention of mutual immediacy is what in the previous section is meant by the term 'everlasting.'

The wisdom of subjective aim prehends every actuality for what it can be in such a perfected system—its sufferings, its sorrows, its failures, its triumphs, its immediacies of joy—woven by rightness of feeling into the harmony of the universal feeling, which is always immediate, always many, always one, always with novel advance, moving onward and never perishing. The revolts of destructive evil, purely self-regarding, are dismissed into their triviality of merely individual facts; and yet the good they did achieve in individual joy, in individual sorrow, in the introduction of needed contrast, is yet saved by its relation to the completed whole. The image—and it is but an image—the image under which this operative growth of God's nature is best conceived, is that of a tender care that nothing be lost.

The consequent nature of God is his judgment on the world. He saves the world as it passes into the immediacy of his own life. It is the judgment of a tenderness which loses nothing that can be saved. It is also the judgment of a wisdom which uses what in the temporal world is mere wreckage.

Another image which is also required to understand his consequent nature, is that of his infinite patience. The universe includes a threefold creative act composed of (i) the one infinite conceptual realization, (ii) the multiple solidarity of free physical realizations in the temporal world, (iii) the ultimate unity of the multiplicity of actual fact with the primordial conceptual fact. If we conceive the first term and the last term in their unity over against the intermediate multiple freedom of physical realizations in the temporal world, we conceive of the patience of God, tenderly saving the turmoil of the intermediate world by the completion of his own nature. The sheer force of things lies in the intermediate physical process: this is the energy of physical production. God's rôle is not the combat of productive force with productive force, of destructive force with destructive force; it lies in the patient operation of the overpowering rationality of his conceptual harmonization. He does not create the world, he saves it: or, more accurately, he is the poet of the world, with tender patience leading it by his vision of truth, beauty, and goodness.

The vicious separation of the flux from the permanence leads to the concept of an entirely static God, with eminent reality, in relation to an entirely fluent world, with deficient reality. But if the opposites, static and fluent, have once been so explained as separately to characterize diverse actualities, the interplay between the thing which is static and the things which are fluent involves contradiction at every step in its explanation. Such philosophies must include the notion of 'illusion' as a fundamental principle—the notion of 'mere appearance.' This is the final platonic problem.

Undoubtedly, the intuitions of Greek, Hebrew, and Christian thought have alike embodied the notions of a static God condescending to the world, and of a world *either* thoroughly fluent, *or* accidentally static, but finally fluent—'heaven and earth shall pass away.' In some schools of thought, the fluency of the world is mitigated by the assumption that selected components in the world are exempt from this final fluency, and achieve a static survival. Such components are not separated by any decisive line from analogous components for which the assumption is not made. Further, the survival is construed in terms of a final pair of opposites, happiness for some, torture for others.

Such systems have the common character of starting with a fundamental intuition which we do mean to express, and of entangling themselves in verbal expressions, which carry consequences at variance with the initial intuition of permanence in fluency and of fluency in permanence.

But civilized intuition has always, although obscurely, grasped the problem as double and not as single. There is not the mere problem of fluency *and* permanence. There is the double problem: actuality with permanence, requiring fluency as its completion; and actuality with fluency, requiring permanence as its completion. The first half of the problem concerns the completion of God's primordial nature by the derivation of his consequent nature from the temporal world. The second half of the problem concerns the completion of each fluent actual occasion by its function of objective immortality, devoid of 'perpetual perishing,' that is to say, 'everlasting.'

This double problem cannot be separated into two distinct problems. Either side can only be explained in terms of the other. The consequent nature of God is the fluent world become 'everlasting' by its objective immortality in God. Also the objective immortality of actual occasions requires the primordial permanence of God, whereby the creative advance ever re-establishes itself endowed with initial subjective aim derived from the relevance of God to the evolving world.

But objective immortality within the temporal world does not solve the problem set by the penetration of the finer religious intuition. 'Everlastingness' has been lost; and 'everlastingness' is the content of that vision upon which the finer religions are built—the 'many' absorbed everlastingly in the final unity. The problems of the fluency of God and of the everlastingness of passing experience are solved by the same factor in the universe. This factor is the temporal world perfected by its reception and its reformation, as a fulfilment of the primordial appetition which is the basis of all order. In this way God is completed by the individual, fluent satisfactions of finite fact, and the temporal occasions are completed by their everlasting union with their transformed selves, purged into conformation with the eternal order which is the final absolute 'wisdom.' The final summary can only be expressed in terms of a group of antitheses, whose apparent self-contradiction depends on neglect of the diverse categories of existence. In each antithesis there is a shift of meaning which converts the opposition into a contrast.

It is as true to say that God is permanent and the World fluent, as that the World is permanent and God is fluent.

It is as true to say that God is one and the World many, as that the World is one and God many.

It is as true to say that, in comparison with the World, God is actual eminently, as that, in comparison with God, the World is actual eminently.

It is as true to say that the World is immanent in God, as that God is immanent in the World.

It is as true to say that God transcends the World, as that the World transcends God.

It is as true to say that God creates the World, as that the World creates God.

God and the World are the contrasted opposites in terms of which Creativity achieves its supreme task of transforming disjoined multiplicity, with its diversities in opposition, into concrescent unity, with its diversities in contrast. In each actuality these are two concrescent poles of realization—'enjoyment' and 'appetition,' that is, the 'physical' and the 'conceptual.' For God the conceptual is prior to the physical, for the World the physical poles are prior to the conceptual poles.

A physical pole is in its own nature exclusive, bounded by contradiction: a conceptual pole is in its own nature all-embracing, unbounded by contradiction. The former derives its share of infinity from the infinity of appetition; the latter derives its share of limitation from the exclusiveness of enjoyment. Thus, by reason of his priority of appetition, there can be but one primordial nature for God; and, by reason of their priority of enjoyment, there must be one history of many actualities in the physical world.

God and the World stand over against each other, expressing the final metaphysical truth that appetitive vision and physical enjoyment have equal claim to priority in creation. But no two actualities can be torn apart: each is all in all. Thus each temporal occasion embodies God, and is embodied in God. In God's nature, permanence is primordial and flux is derivative from the World: in the World's nature, flux is primordial and permanence is derivative from God. Also the World's nature is a primordial datum for God; and God's nature is a primordial datum for the World. Creation achieves the reconciliation of permanence and flux when it has reached its final term which is everlastingness—the Apotheosis of the World.

Opposed elements stand to each other in mutual requirement. In their unity, they inhibit or contrast. God and the World stand to each other in this opposed requirement. God is the infinite ground of all mentality, the unity of vision seeking physical multiplicity. The World is the multiplicity of finites, actualities seeking a perfected unity. Neither God, nor the World, reaches static completion. Both are in the grip of the ultimate metaphysical ground, the creative advance into novelty. Either of them, God and the World, is the instrument of novelty for the other.

PART III

God and the World Religions

JOACHIM WACH

Universals in Religion

Joachim Wach was born in Germany in 1898 and educated chiefly at the University of Leipzig. During this time he came under the influence of Husserl, Rudolf Otto, and Heiler. In 1935 Wach's appointment at Leipzig was terminated under the Nazi regime. Through a friend he was invited to Brown University, where he taught until 1945 when he went to the University of Chicago. Wach's main interests were the history of religions and the philosophical analysis of religious experience. A man of great learning, Wach contributed much to the comparative study of religions and was much concerned to relate Christianity to the Eastern religions. Wach wrote many books in German; he was best known in America for his Sociology of Religion (1944) *and* The Comparative Study of Religions (1958). *He died in 1955.*

The careful research of many a generation of scholars, the travel reports, not only of adventurers, missionaries and explorers, but of many a person you and I count among our personal acquaintances, have brought home to well-nigh all of us a realization of the variety of religious ideas and practices that exist in the world. The result of this realization has been bewilderment and confusion in many hearts and minds. Roughly three different types of reaction to the situation can be discerned: (i) scepticism, that is, the refusal to see in all these religious ideas and usages more than the expression of ignorance and folly, in other words a cultural and/or religious 'lag'; (ii) relativism, that is, a disposition to dispense with the problem of truth in favour of a non-committal registration of all there is and has been, an attitude which has found much favour in the latter-day circles of scholars and intellectuals; and finally (iii) the desire to investigate the variety of what goes under the names of religion and religions in order to determine by comparison and phenomenological analysis if anything like a structure can be discovered in all these forms of expression, to what kind of experiences this variegated expression can be traced, and finally, what kind of reality or realities may correspond to the experiences in question. It is the

Reprinted from *Types of Religious Experience* by Joachim Wach by permission of The University of Chicago Press, pp. 30–34. Copyright 1951 by The University of Chicago Press.

83

last of the three types of reaction to the predicament characterized above which seems to us the only promising and fruitful one, and we propose to follow it in what we have to say here.

The first difficulty we encounter in trying to bring some order into the bewildering mass of material that geography, anthropology, sociology, archaeology, philology, history, and the history of religions have placed at our disposal, is the need for criteria which would enable us to distinguish between what is religious and what is not. Now you will not expect me to discuss the well-nigh endless series of definitions of religion which have been proposed by the great and the not-so-great during recent decades. We shall also find it impossible to use as our yardstick one of the classical historical formulations evolved in one of the great religious communities itself, say in the Christian. For we should soon discover that it is not possible to identify religion with what we have come to know as Christian or Jewish or Hindu, even if we forget for the moment that it would be far from easy to agree on which of the available formulations we want to use. Some of us might feel, at first thought, that it is after all not so difficult to determine what may be called religious and what is not religious; they would point to the neat divisions which we are accustomed to find in our text-books, dealing with the lives of individuals, societies and cultures, past and present, in which separate chapters deal with man's political views and activities, his economic situation, his interest in the arts, and his religious orientation, or with the social organization, the economics, the legal institutions, the arts and sciences, the moral life, and the religion of a given tribe, people or nation. But, on second thoughts, the unsatisfactory character of such parcelling becomes evident; and that not only in the repetitions and omissions which this procedure entails. No wonder then that some investigators—and we find among them distinguished anthropologists, philosophers, and theologians—have come to the conclusion that religion is not anything distinct and *sui generis,* but is a name given to the sum of man's aspirations, to the whole of the civilization of a people. If we reject this view, it is not because we want to separate sharply between religion on the one hand and on the other all that makes up an individual's or a society's other experiences and activities. But we are of the opinion that, in order to be able to assess the interrelation and interpenetration of the various interests, attitudes, and activities of man, we have to examine very carefully the nature of his propensities, drives, impulses, actions, and reactions. William James has rightly said: 'The essence of religious experiences, the thing by which we must finally judge them, must be that element or quality in them which we can meet nowhere else. We disagree with those who are prone to identify religion with just one segment of man's inner existence: feeling, willing, or cogitating. In order to lay down our criteria, we cannot be satisfied to examine only the conceptually articulated perceptions or only the emotions and affections and the respective expressions in which they have become manifest. We propose rather the following *four formal criteria* for a definition of what might be called religious experience:

1. Religious experience is a response to what is experienced as ultimate reality; that is, in religious experiences we react not to any single or finite phenomenon, material or otherwise, but to what we realize as undergirding and conditioning all that constitutes our world of experiences. We agree with Paul Tillich when he says that 'the presence of the demand of "ultimacy" in the structure of our existence is the basis of religious experience'. Before him William James said in his book on the *Varieties of Religious Experience*— a passage quoted in Paul Johnson's *Psychology of Religion:* 'It is as if there were in the human consciousness a sense of reality, a feeling of objective presence, a perception of what we may call "something there," more deep and more general than any of the special and particular "senses" by which the current psychology supposes existent realities to be originally revealed'. Or as the author of a recent textbook on Psychology of Religion formulates it: 'Religious experience is response to stimuli that represent an active reality viewed as divine, or as creative of values.'

This response has the tendency to persist, once communion with the source of life and values is established, and man is restless to reassure himself of its continuance.

2. Religious experience is a total response of the total being to what is apprehended as ultimate reality. That is, we are involved not exclusively with our mind, our affections, or our will, but as integral persons.

3. Religious experience is the most intense experience of which man is capable. That is not to say that all expression of religious experience testifies to this intensity but that, potentially, genuine religious experience is of this nature, as is instanced in conflicts between different basic drives or motivations. Religious loyalty, if it

is religious loyalty, wins over all other loyalties. The modern term 'existential' designates the profound concern and the utter seriousness of this experience.

4. Religious experience is practical, that is to say it involves an imperative, a commitment which impels man to act. This activistic note distinguishes it from aesthetic experience, of which it shares the intensity, and joins it with moral experience. Moral judgment, however, does not necessarily represent a reaction to ultimate reality.

It should be borne in mind that one, two, or three of these criteria would not suffice to reassure us that we are dealing with genuine religious experience. All four would have to be present. If they are, we should have no difficulty in distinguishing between religious and non-religious experiences. However, there are *pseudo-religious* and *semi-religious* experiences. The former are non-religious and known to be such to the person or persons who pretend to them by using forms of expression peculiar to religion. The latter may show the presence of the second, third and fourth characteristics, but refer not to ultimate but to some aspect of 'finite' reality. The intense and possibly sacrificial devotion with which somebody may 'worship' a loved person, his race, his social group, or his state are instances of semi-religious loyalties. Because they are directed toward finite values, they are idolatrous rather than religious.

Now it is our contention, and this is the first proposition in regard to our topic, that religious experience, as we have just attempted to define it by means of these four criteria, is *universal*. The empirical proof of this statement can be found in the testimonies of explorers and investigators. 'There are no peoples, however primitive, without religion and magic,' is the opening sentence of one of Malinowski's well-known essays. In practically all cases where a rash negative conclusion has been reached, more careful research has corrected the initial error.

A *second* proposition is this: religious experience tends towards *expression*. This tendency is universal. Only in and through its expression does any of our experiences exist for others, does any religious experience exist for us, the students of the history of religion. The religious experience of another person can never become the object of direct observation. Some important hermeneutical consequences result from the recognition of this fact.

Now for the *third* step in our search for universals in religion. A comparative study of the *forms* of the expression of religious experience, the world over, shows an amazing similarity in structure. We should like to summarize the result of such comparative studies by the statement: all expression of religious experience falls under the three headings of *theoretical expression, practical expression,* and *sociological expression.* Everywhere and at all times man has felt the need to articulate his religious experience in three ways: conceptually; by action, or practically; and in covenanting, or sociologically. There is no religion deserving of the name in which any one of these three elements is totally lacking, though the degree and, of course, the tempo of this development may vary. Notwithstanding numerous attempts at establishing priority for one of these three modes of expression, we feel that it would be futile to argue that myth precedes cult or that both precede fellowship: history teaches us that the dynamics of religious life is made up of the interpenetration of these three aspects.

WILLIAM ERNEST HOCKING

Christianity and the Problem of a World Faith

William Ernest Hocking was born in 1873 and studied philosophy under James, Palmer, Royce, and Santayana at Harvard. Hocking was for many years Alford Professor of Philosophy at Harvard, having succeeded Royce in that post upon the latter's death in 1916. An early student of Husserl and of phenomenology, Hocking made a unique synthesis of radical empiricism and idealism developing his views in a number of well-known books. His systematic philosophy of religion is found in The Meaning of God in Human Experience (1912; 2d ed., 1963). His political philosophy is contained in Man and the State (1926). A prolific writer, Hocking belongs to the comprehensive tradition in philosophy, where the emphasis falls on including every aspect of experience within the unity of a synoptic vision. Other works include What Man Can Make of Man (1940), The Coming World Civilization (1956), and The Meaning of Immortality in Human Experience (1957).

We cannot forget that the origin of [Christianity] was in a stupendous effort to pass from the external and intricate corpus of a highly developed religious system to its central spirit. The opposition which the Teacher aroused was due not to new notions which he introduced, but to existing ones which he declared unessential, and to the personal authority which he claimed in making his drastic revaluations. It was the essence of Judaism which he sought—"for this is the law and the prophets"—but what he found was a core of faith which seekers after God under all names and none could recognize as answering their unspoken meaning.

Even in the trappings we have made for it, something of its native clarity shines through with emancipating force. Hu Shih regards himself as a naturalist philosopher and a critic of all organised religion, especially of those other-worldly types from which China has had so much to suffer; yet it is Hu Shih who, looking at Christianity as a phenomenon in China, judges that it is relatively free from

From William Ernest Hocking, Living Religions and a World Faith (London: George Allen & Unwin, Ltd., 1940), pp. 231–233; 254–263. Used by permission of the publisher.

superstition and demands a relative purity of life; further, that the transitional misfits which it produces are not to be too severely censured, since in any period of new orientation, and weaning from the past, such moods must occur.[1] Wherever it goes, Christianity tends to serve as a clarifying agency, reducing the complexities and extraneous loads of religion, giving the human mind a property in its world-view, and an insight into the meaning of the will of God, freeing the human will from the burden of opaque acceptance.

But note, too, that this "simple essence" we speak of is not limited to the teaching of the Sermon on the Mount. It is the great gain of the present moment in history that the emerging faith has come, in the way we have traced, upon the human sense of the idea of incarnation. This mystery has become to just this extent generally intelligible—a quality rightly regarded in theological quarters with suspicion, yet not necessarily treasonable! And with this gain the meaning of Christianity has become much more accessible to mankind at large.

Men have always been ready to do homage to the teachings of Jesus, as beautiful statements of an impracticable ideal. They are prepared to incorporate these ideals in their own codes. They have halted at the doctrine of "the divine Word made flesh." They have not seen that without the entrance of deity into human life the Sermon on the Mount can neither be practised nor understood. Hence the radicalism of that Sermon remains to them poetry, an extravagance, fanatical; it refuses to connect with conduct, draws down the just reproach of the Moslem and the Hindu that it is beyond reach, leaves Christendom itself with a divided conscience if not a besetting hypocrisy. . . .

What the values in the other religions are, which Christianity does not have, is a matter whose precise determination may never be finished. Perhaps it is not capable of a wholly objective answer. I can certainly not pretend here to give such an answer. But I may give a report of my personal judgments, as I have found here and there is the world expressions of the spirit of the non-Christian religions at their best.

[1] Conversation, 1932. Here I am moved to quote Dean Inge's citation of Bishop Hall, a seventeenth-century divine, who said that "the most useful of all books on theology would be one with the title, De Paucitate Credendorum, or the fewness of the things which a man must believe."—*Things New and Old*, 1933, p. 48.

Islam.—Within Islam one is aware of a dignity, a sweep, a sense of the instant majesty of God, which we lack. Among Islamic peoples one sees how the habitual thought about God becomes a part of the personal quality of the man; dignity enters into him also. None of these concepts are lacking to us; nor have they failed to find their way into architecture and music. But they lack saliency in our religious expression and in our lives.

To the Moslem, God in His majesty is also a near and present God. Our mediators aid, and also impede; when we make them objects of worship, they carry a descent. The Moslem never forgets that it is God with whom he has to do. If his escape from the intermediate clutter leaves him stark, it also clarifies his soul.

Islam has also an effective fraternity which crosses racial bounds with an ease which Christianity professes but Christians seldom attain. The solidarity and unimpressionableness of Islam are largely due to the fact that Islam has no proletariat. The book is open to all on the same terms—at least in Arabic; it is the school book of the whole Moslem world. Beneath the sects, the simplicity of the central confession, and the felt pettiness of human distinctions in the sight of Allah, weld its people into a religious unity not realised elsewhere.

Hinduism and Buddhism.— . . . In general, these religions are weak in respect to history, and require the supplement of the Semitic genius. But the need is mutual.

The relief from literalness of the conceptual treatment of religion, in these Indian traditions, is towards mysticism and poetry rather than towards history. The advantage is that poetry and myth are seldom in danger of being confused with reason. In the Semitic religions, the line between narrative and myth is not clear; and the consequence is that western Christianity has never been sure which is its poetry and which its prose. Our persistent loyalties to myth in the guise of history give western Christianity a distinctly stupid and childish air, as compared with the inlighted deftness of touch of the true oriental, especially the Indian mind.

I would mention, too, the naturalness of the meditative element of religion, so that school children know instinctively what is to be done in an hour of "meditation." The psychological principle is accepted that a price must be paid for insight: it is not to be had in the intervals of a packed school-programme; efficiency is a misapprehension of the meaning of the need to realize a thought: time, preparation, and effort must be spent in order to see.

And while, as has been well pointed out, the spirituality of the East dare not ignore the genuine spirituality involved in the intrepid drive for truth characteristic of western science, the fundamental ethical discipline of the empirical attitude, it remains true that there is another facet of spirituality still pre-eminently oriental—the willingness among all groups, and not alone among the devotees, to pay the price of spiritual gifts, the capacity to renounce the lesser for the greater.

Christianity is right in locating its life in both worlds, and in refusing to count illusory or evil the apparent reals and goods of the surface of experience; they, too, are the garment of God—or better, the moment-by-moment doings of God. But in its joy at this discovery, it is easily seduced by its own comfort. It too easily takes "prosperity" as a sign of the favour of God, and the harvest festival of thanksgiving as the highest moment of its prayer, the prayer over a heavy meal. The Orient is less a despiser of this world than repute has accused it of being, but it more instantly realizes the insidious hold of physical enjoyment on the proportions of moral sanity; and more promptly renounces, with large and magnanimous thoroughness, what it discovers to be a personal peril to the soul.

There remains a third point of excellence: the actually achieved serenity of spirit in many an oriental saint.

It is no idle boast when one of these men gives an affirmative answer to the question, Have you found peace? The old Stoic ideal of the imperturbable man is more frequently realized in India, I surmise, than in any other part of the world to-day, because with the actuality of renunciation there follows at once a freedom from petty fears, from angers, and from anxiety about many things. Compared with the discreditable and unchristian agitation of Christian leaders here and there over the menace of communism or the general state of the world, and the shameful hurry-up campaigns for world-conquest by Christianity, these quietly-great souls may well be a means of ushering Christianity into a region of its own proper meaning.

Buddhism.—In Buddhism I would especially mention a matter which is likely to stir emotions of apprehension in a Christian mind.

I mean the enjoyment of the *impersonal element* of ultimate truth.

In my own belief, personality is the deeper and more inclusive category. For a person is capable of entertaining the impersonal, whereas the impersonal has no capacity of itself for entertaining the personal. A person may, for example, school himself to be more like a law of nature, and less subject to whimsical variations of mood; whereas a law of nature has no capacity for developing the quality of personality!

But impersonality belongs, as it were, to the vast inner spaces of God's being. The inability to trust oneself to the enjoyment of the impersonal regularities of the world whether of science or of the moral law—as if regularity, which gives hold to science, must therefore be hostile to religion (as giving a proof of self-operation!), betrays a lack of faith in God and a certain pettiness of religious conception from which the better minds of the Orient are quite free.

Buddhism, in its origins, no doubt tended to err in the other direction, and too fully swept away the personal element which might still be clinging to the notion of the absolute substance, in the interest of absolute law of process; and has, in the dialectic of its own long history been led to compensate for that fault in the growing predominance of the Bodhisattva conceptions, and especially of Amida Buddha, the gracious. But one must still keep open the question whether the corrections have improved the case; in so far as personal deities introduce an opportunist element into the relations of God and man, religion is cheapened rather than enlarged.

It is more easy for Indian than for Christian piety to recognise that the pursuit of truth is a part of the love of God (in Gandhi's view, tending to identity). The Platonic Ideas of Beauty and Goodness are not at once, by the Christian mind, perceived to have anything to do with religion, still less to be ingredients of the nature of God; and loyalty to abstract causes, such as justice or liberty in some specific shape, is likely to take on a purely secular ring. This is partly due to the long struggle of early Christianity with the menace of a Platonism which would have eaten the heart out of its historical concreteness; the battle was rightly decided against the Platonists. But Christianity still suffers from the iniquity of making this a party issue; it remains semi-blind to the majesty of the impersonal element in the being of God, and hence misjudges its own scope.

Confucianism.—It is a very opposite excellence that we find here, namely, its intense humanity. The "filial piety" from which Confucius undertook to deduce the whole duty of man, is based on the assumption that the family tie is at the same time a sacred tie; the family, as an over-personal entity, receiving the spirits of its own dead and continuing their connection with the living, being for its members the nearest medium of access to the heavenly sphere, and the most constantly invoked. That this relationship has been an impediment to progress, as it has been interpreted, no one sees more clearly than the Confucianist of to-day. But that it need be a bar to progress he is ready to deny; and that the new China has need of it he rightly insists. The family organisation changes, the large family dissolves, the exclusive loyalty to all things in the universe via the family is widening into other recognitions, national and abstract. But the obligation of the family to its members, for their education in the moral elements of life, and of its members to it on account of that transmissive function, is as vital to the new China as to the old, and as vital to the new Occident as to the Orient.

The family, like the state, must prepare for its own supercession. It must produce the free individual, and in him risk the loss of its own fabric; for it is only the free individual that can preserve that fabric. China has to learn with pain the secret of the inner strength of the non-communistic schemes of personal life. But the vast inner moral resources of China under present strains may show that her traditional system of "sacred relationships" has been so interpreted as to leave much initiative and self-judgment available as a national resource. The human bonds are destined to give strength to the individual, not to submerge him. And it is this which we in our western skittishness, and rooted distrust of group presumptions, have still to appreciate. If the human bond is veritably a way to God, whether through the modestly estimated virtues of the ancestors—about which the Chinese were little given to effusiveness—or through revulsions against their vices, it is cured, or has in itself the potential cure, of its tyranny.

If the human bond to parents sets itself up as an Absolute it may be reminded, as President Lim would remind it, that parents and ancestors are to be revered *only so far as they are worthy of reverence!* It is the function of the valid Absolute to keep all relatives reminded of their relativity. With this in mind the Chinese conception of the human bonds as mediator of the divine becomes significant for all religion, not excluding Christianity.

I would also mention the prevalent cheerfulness and naturalness of the Confucian conception of religion; one might speak of its inner gaiety.

This is sometimes ascribed to a Chinese deficiency in the sense of sin, the peculiar grace which gives to Christianity its deep disturbing, chastening and therefore rebuilding power. And I quite agree that contrition is a sign of depth, provided it comes without being worked for. The question is, however, not whether any person or race is sufficiently depressed in view of its defectiveness, but whether it is capable of perceiving the ideal at all; for if it perceives the ideal and is self-conscious, the judgment of its distance from perfection is not escapable, nor the question of what it can do to be cured. In itself, the perception of the ideal is a joy; and the normal attitude of the Christian is not one of despair, but one of gratitude that he has recognised the standard which at once condemns him and exalts him. In this normal attitude, it is not unlikely that China, which is not deficient in its sense of the standard, may still have something to teach us. For gaiety also is not without its route to holiness, as Gilbert Chesterton saw when he wrote his phrase, "the giant laughter of Christian men." [2]

I do not suggest that these impressions of mine touch even the most important of the idiosyncrasies of non-Christian faiths. I mention them somewhat at random as characteristics which may typify the problem which Christianity as a world-faith would have to meet. No religion could present itself as the completion of other faiths until it had gone through the labour of understanding those faiths. And this labour no religion has as yet more than begun. The proposition that "Jesus Christ includes everything," however valuable as a postulate of faith to be made good by the thoughtful effort of the believer, when set up as an *a priori* basis for the intercourse of religions is simply unacceptable. It is right, and indeed necessary, for the good of men, that the non-Christian religions should hold to their own, at least until they find themselves in fact understood, translated, and included in the growing power of a religion which in achieving its own full potentiality, achieves theirs also.

[2] Ballad of the White Horse.

PAUL TILLICH

The Encounter Between Religions

Paul Tillich was born in Germany in 1886 and came to America in 1933 after having been dismissed from his post as Professor of Philosophy in Frankfurt by the Nazi regime. Since that time Tillich has taught and lectured in America, first as Professor of Philosophical Theology at Union Theological Seminary until his retirement in 1956 and later as University Professor at Harvard University. In 1950 he was Terry Lecturer at Yale University. Tillich is at present lecturing at the University of Chicago. He is one of the most important and influential theologians alive today, striving to keep up the dialogue between philosophy and theology through his system of "philosophical theology." Author of many books, including the three-volume Systematic Theology (1951–1963), The Courage To Be (1950), The Protestant Era (1948), Love, Power and Justice (1954), Dynamics of Faith (1957), Morality and Beyond (1963), Tillich brings to bear the insights of existential philosophy and depth psychology for the contemporary reinterpretation of classical Christian doctrines.

Christianity had encountered mysticism long before the modern opening up of India. A decisive struggle was made against Julian the Apostate's ideas of a restitution of paganism with the help of Neoplatonic mysticism. When we look at this struggle we find, on both sides, arguments similar to those used in our contemporary encounters with Indian mysticism. The Christian theologians were and are right in criticizing the nonpersonal, nonsocial and nonhistorical attitude of the mystical religions, but they had to accept the countercriticism of the mystical groups that their own personalism is primitive and needs interpretation in transpersonal terms. This has been at least partly accepted by Christian theologians who, in agreement with the long line of Christian mystics, have asserted that without a mystical element—namely, an experience of the immediate presence of the divine—there is no religion at all. . . .

If Christianity rejects the idea that it is a religion, it must fight in itself everything by which it becomes a religion. With some justification one can say that the two essential expressions of religion

From Paul Tillich, Christianity and the Encounter of the World Religions (New York: Columbia University Press, 1963), pp. 88–97. Reprinted with permission of the Columbia University Press.

in the narrower sense are myth and cult. If Christianity fights against itself as a religion it must fight against myth and cult, and this it has done. It did so in the Bible, which, one should not forget, is not only a religious but also an antireligious book. The Bible fights for God against religion. This fight is rather strong in the Old Testament, where it is most powerful in the attack of the prophets against the cult and the polytheistic implications of the popular religion. In harsh criticism the whole Israelitic cult is rejected by some early prophets, and so is the mythology which gives the national gods ultimate validity. The God of Israel has been "demythologized" into the God of the universe, and the gods of the nations are "nothings." The God of Israel rejects even Israel in the moment when she claims Him as a national god. God denies His being *a* god.

The same fight against cult and myth is evident in the New Testament. The early records of the New Testament are full of stories in which Jesus violates ritual laws in order to exercise love, and in Paul the whole ritual law is dispossessed by the appearance of the Christ. John adds demythologization to deritualization: the eternal life is here and now, the divine judgment is identical with the acceptance or rejection of the light which shines for everybody. The early church tried to demythologize the idea of God and the meaning of the Christ by concepts taken from the Platonic-Stoic tradition. In all periods theologians tried hard to show the transcendence of the divine over the finite symbols expressing him. The idea of "God above God" (the phrase I used in *The Courage To Be*) can be found implicitly in all patristic theology. Their encounter with pagan polytheism, i.e., with gods on a finite basis, made the Church Fathers extremely sensitive to any concept which would present God as being analogous to the gods of those against whom they were fighting. Today this particular encounter, namely with polytheism, no longer has manifest reality; therefore the theologians have become careless in safeguarding their idea of a personal God from slipping into "henotheistic" mythology (the belief in *one* god who, however, remains particular and bound to a particular group).

The early theologians were supported by the mystical element which in the fifth century became a powerful force in Christianity. The main concept of mysticism is immediacy: immediate participation in the divine Ground by elevation into unity with it, transcending all finite realities and all finite symbols of the divine, leaving the sacramental activities far below and sinking cult and myth into the experienced abyss of the Ultimate. Like the prophetical and the theological critique, this is an attack against religion for the sake of religion.

The ritual element was devaluated by the Reformation, in the theology of both the great reformers and of the evangelical radicals. One of the most cutting attacks of Luther was directed against the *vita religiosa,* the life of the *homini religiosi,* the monks. God is present in the secular realm; in this view Renaissance and Reformation agree. It was an important victory in the fight of God against religion.

The Enlightenment brought a radical elimination of myth and cult. What was left was a philosophical concept of God as the bearer of the moral imperative. Prayer was described by Kant as something of which a reasonable man is ashamed if surprised in it. Cult and myth disappear in the philosophy of the eighteenth century, and the Church is redefined by Kant as a society with moral purposes.

All this is an expression of the religious or quasi-religious fight against religion. But the forces which were fighting to preserve Christianity as a religion were ultimately stronger, in defense and counterattack. The main argument used in the counterattacks is the observation that the loss of cult and myth is the loss of the revelatory experience on which every religion is based. Such experience needs self-expression to continue, and that means it needs mythical and ritual elements. Actually they are never lacking. They are present in every religion and quasi-religion, even in their most secularized forms. An existential protest against myth and cult is possible only in the power of myth and cult. All attacks against them have a religious background, which they try to conceal, but without success. We know today what a secular myth is. We know what a secular cult is. The totalitarian movements have provided us with both. Their great strength was that they transformed ordinary concepts, events, and persons into myths, and ordinary performances into rituals; therefore they had to be fought with other myths and rituals—religious and secular. You cannot escape them, however you demythologize and deritualize. They always return and you must always judge them again. In the fight of God against religion the fighter for God is in the paradoxical situation that he has to use religion in order to fight religion.

It is a testimony to present-day Christianity that it is aware of this situation. We have mentioned the opposition to the concept of religion in the philosophy of religion as one of the symptoms of this fight. We have used the word demythologize. We have used the term quasi-religion to indicate that man's ultimate concern can express itself in secular terms. We find contemporary theologians (like Bonhöffer martyred by the Nazis) maintaining that Christianity must become secular, and that God is present in what we do as citizens, as creative artists, as friends, as lovers of nature, as workers in a profession, so that it may have eternal meaning. Christianity for these men has become an expression of the ultimate meaning in the actions of our daily life. And this is what it should be.

And now we have to ask: What is the consequence of this judgment of Christianity of itself for its dealing with the world religions? We have seen, first of all, that it is a mutual judging which opens the way for a fair valuation of the encountered religions and quasi-religions.

Such an attitude prevents contemporary Christianity from attempting to "convert" in the traditional and depreciated sense of this word. Many Christians feel that it is a questionable thing, for instance, to try to convert Jews. They have lived and spoken with their Jewish friends for decades. They have not converted them, but they have created a community of conversation which has changed both sides of the dialogue. Some day this ought to happen also with people of Islamic faith. Most attempts to convert them have failed, but we may try to reach them on the basis of their growing insecurity in face of the secular world, and they may come to self-criticism in analogy to our own self-criticism.

Finally, in relation to Hinduism, Buddhism, and Taoism, we should continue the dialogue which has already started. . . . Not conversion, but dialogue. It would be a tremendous step forward if Christianity were to accept this! It would mean that Christianity would judge itself when it judges the others in the present encounter of the world religions.

But it would do even more. It would give a new valuation to secularism. The attack of secularism on all present-day religions would not appear as something merely negative. If Christianity denies itself as a religion, the secular development could be understood in a new sense, namely as the indirect way which historical destiny takes to unite mankind religiously, and this would mean, if we include the quasi-religions, also politically. When we look at the formerly pagan, now Communist, peoples, we may venture the idea that the secularization of the main groups of present-day mankind may be the way to their religious transformation.

This leads to the last and most universal problem of our subject: Does our analysis demand either a mixture of religions or the victory of one religion, or the end of the religious age altogether? We answer: None of these alternatives! A mixture of religions destroys in each of them the concreteness which gives it its dynamic power. The victory of *one* religion would impose a particular religious answer on all other particular answers. The end of the religious age—one has already spoken of the end of the Christian or the Protestant age—is an impossible concept. The religious principle cannot come to an end. For the question of the ultimate meaning of life cannot be silenced as long as men are men. Religion cannot come to an end, and a particular religion will be lasting to the degree in which it negates itself as a religion. Thus Christianity will be a bearer of the religious answer as long as it breaks through its own particularity.

The way to achieve this is not to relinquish one's religious tradition for the sake of a universal concept which would be nothing but a concept. The way is to penetrate into the depth of one's own religion, in devotion, thought and action. In the depth of every living religion there is a point at which the religion itself loses its importance, and that to which it points breaks through its particularity, elevating it to spiritual freedom and with it to a vision of the spiritual presence in other expressions of the ultimate meaning of man's existence.

This is what Christianity must see in the present encounter of the world religions.

Same
one

022.3

PART IV
God and Philosophy

G. W. F. HEGEL

The Identity of Philosophy and Religion

Hegel was born in Stuttgart in 1770. As Professor of Philosophy first at Heidelberg and later at Berlin, Hegel was the most important influence on continental philosophy throughout the nineteenth century. With the aid of his dialectical method he set forth a vast system of categories intended to express the true nature of everything that is. Hegel's Absolute Idealism is the view that Spirit in the sense of self-conscious thought alone is real. According to Hegel, reality is thoroughly transparent to spirit and can be known as a coherent system. All features of human life and experience were interpreted by Hegel from his idealist standpoint—law and morality, religion and art, philosophy and natural science. A student of theology, Hegel never lost sight of the close connection between the metaphysical and the religious issues. His most important works are The Phenomenology of Mind *(trans. Baillie, 1910),* The Logic *from the* Encyclopedia *(trans., Wallace, 1892),* Philosophy of Mind *from the* Encyclopedia *(trans., Wallace, 1894),* Philosophy of Right *(trans., Knox, 1942),* The Science of Logic *(trans. Johnston and Struthers, 1929).* Hegel died in 1831.*

In saying above that philosophy makes religion the subject of consideration, and when further this consideration of it appears to be in the position of something which is different from its object, it would seem as if we are still occupying that attitude in which both sides remain mutually independent and separate. In taking up such an attitude in thus considering the subject, we should accordingly come out of that region of devotion and enjoyment which religion is, and the object and the consideration of it as the movement of thought would be as different as, for example, the geometrical figures in mathematics are from the mind which considers them. Such is only the relation, however, as it at first appears, when knowledge is still severed from the religious side, and is finite knowledge. On the contrary, when we look more closely, it becomes apparent that as a matter of fact the content, the need, and the interest of philosophy represent something which it has in common with religion.

The object of religion as well as of philosophy is eternal truth in

From G. W. F. Hegel, *Lectures on the Philosophy of Religion* (trans. Rev. E. B. Speirs and J. B. Sanderson; London: Routledge & Kegan Paul, 1895), Vol. I, pp. 18–25.

its objectivity, God and nothing but God, and the explication of God. Philosophy is not a wisdom of the world, but is knowledge of what is not of the world; it is not knowledge which concerns external mass, or empirical existence and life, but is knowledge of that which is eternal, of what God is, and what flows out of His nature. For this His nature must reveal and develop itself. Philosophy, therefore, only unfolds itself when it unfolds religion, and in unfolding itself it unfolds religion. As thus occupied with eternal truth which exists on its own account, or is in and for itself, and, as in fact, a dealing on the part of the thinking spirit, and not of individual caprice and particular interest, with this object, it is the same kind of activity as religion is. The mind in so far as it thinks philosophically immerses itself with like living interest in this object, and renounces its particularity in that it permeates its object, in the same way, as religious consciousness does, for the latter also does not seek to have anything of its own, but desires only to immerse itself in this content.

Thus religion and philosophy come to be one. Philosophy is itself, in fact, worship; it is religion, for in the same way it renounces subjective notions and opinions in order to occupy itself with God. Philosophy is thus identical with religion, but the distinction is that it is so in a peculiar manner, distinct from the manner of looking at things which is commonly called religion as such. What they have in common is, that they are religion; what distinguishes them from each other is merely the kind and manner of religion we find in each. It is in the peculiar way in which they both occupy themselves with God that the distinction comes out. It is just here, however, that the difficulties lie which appear so great, that it is even regarded as an impossibility that philosophy should be one with religion. Hence comes the suspicion with which philosophy is looked upon by theology, and the antagonistic attitude of religion and philosophy. In accordance with this antagonistic attitude (as theology considers it to be) philosophy seems to act injuriously, destructively, upon religion, robbing it of its sacred character, and the way in which it occupies itself with God seems to be absolutely different from religion. Here, then, is the same old opposition and contradiction which had already made its appearance among the Greeks. Among that free democratic people, the Athenians, philosophical writings were burnt, and Socrates was condemned to death; now, however, this opposition is held to be an acknowledged fact, more so than that unity of religion and philosophy just asserted.

Old though this opposition is, however, the combination of philosophy and religion is just as old. Already to the neo-Pythagoreans and neo-Platonists, who were as yet within the heathen world, the gods of the people were not gods of imagination, but had become gods of thought. That combination had a place, too, among the most eminent of the Fathers of the Church, who in their religious life took up an essentially intellectual attitude inasmuch as they set out from the presupposition that theology is religion together with conscious thought and comprehension. It is to their philosophical culture that the Christian Church is indebted for the first beginnings of a content of Christian doctrine.

This union of religion and philosophy was carried out to a still greater extent in the Middle Ages. So little was it believed that the knowledge which seeks to comprehend is hurtful to faith, that it was even held to be essential to the further development of faith itself. It was by setting out from philosophy that those great men, Anselm and Abelard, further developed the essential characteristics of faith.

Knowledge in constructing its world for itself, without reference to religion, had only taken possession of the finite contents; but since it has developed into the true philosophy, it has the same content as religion.

If we now look provisionally for the distinction between religion and philosophy as it presents itself in this unity of content, we find it takes the following form:—

a. A speculative philosophy is the consciousness of the Idea, so that everything is apprehended as Idea; the Idea, however, is the True in thought, and not in mere sensuous contemplation or in ordinary conception. The True in thought, to put it more precisely, means that it is something concrete, posited as divided in itself, and in such a way, indeed, that the two sides of what is divided are *opposed characteristics of thought,* and the Idea must be conceived of as the unity of these. To think speculatively means to resolve anything real into its parts, and to oppose these to each other in such a way that the distinctions are set in opposition in accordance with the characteristics of thought, and the object is apprehended as unity of the two.

In sense-perception or picture-thought we have the object before us as a whole, our reflection distinguishes, apprehends different sides, recognises the diversity in them, and severs them. In this act of distinguishing, reflection does not keep firm hold of their unity.

Sometimes it forgets the wholeness, sometimes the distinctions; and if it has both before it, it yet separates the properties from the object, and so places both that that in which the two are one becomes a third, which is different from the object and its properties. In the case of mechanical objects which appear in the region of externality, this relation may have a place, for the object is only the lifeless substratum for the distinctions, and the quality of oneness is the gathering together of external aggregates. In the true object, however, which is not merely an aggregate, an externally united multiplicity, the object is one, although it has characteristics which are distinguished from it, and it is speculative thought which first gets a grasp of the unity in this very antithesis as such. It is in fact the business of speculative thought to apprehend all objects of pure thought, of nature and of Spirit, in the form of thought, and thus as the unity of the difference.

b. Religion, then, is itself the standpoint of the consciousness of the True, which is in and for itself, and is consequently the stage of Spirit at which the speculative content generally, is object for consciousness. Religion is not consciousness of this or that truth in individual objects, but of the absolute truth, of truth as the Universal, the All-comprehending, outside of which there lies nothing at all. The content of its consciousness is further the Universally True, which exists on its own account or in and for itself, which determines itself, and is not determined from without. While the finite required an Other for its determinateness, the True has its determinateness, the limit, its end in itself; it is not limited through an Other, but the Other is found in itself. It is this speculative element which comes to consciousness in religion. Truth is, indeed, contained in every other sphere, but not the highest absolute truth, for this exists only in perfect universality of characterisation or determination, and in the fact of being determined in and for itself, which is not simple determinateness having reference to an Other, but contains the Other, the difference in its very self.

c. Religion is accordingly this speculative element in the form, as it were, of a state of consciousness, of which the aspects are not simple qualities of thought, but are concretely filled up. These moments can be no other than the moment of Thought, active universality, thought in operation, and reality as immediate, particular self-consciousness.

Now, while in philosophy the rigidity of these two sides loses itself through reconciliation in thought, because both sides are thoughts, and the one is not pure universal thought, and the other of an empirical and individual character, religion only arrives at the enjoyment of unity by lifting these two rigid extremes out of this state of severance, by rearranging them, and bringing them together again. But by thus stripping off the form of dualism from its extremes, rendering the opposition in the element of Universality fluid, and bringing it to reconciliation, religion remains always akin to thought, even in its form and movement; and philosophy, as simply active thought, and thought which unites opposed elements, has approached closely to religion.

The contemplation of religion in thought has thus raised the determinate moments of religion to the rank of thoughts, and the question is how this contemplation of religion in thought is related generally to philosophy as forming an organic part in its system.

a. In philosophy, the Highest is called the Absolute, the Idea; it is superfluous to go further back here, and to mention that this Highest was in the Wolfian Philosophy called *ens,* Thing; for that at once proclaims itself an abstraction, which corresponds very inadequately to our idea of God. In the more recent philosophy, the Absolute is not so complete an abstraction, but yet it has not on that account the same signification as is implied in the term, God. In order even to make the difference apparent, we must in the first place consider what the word signify itself signifies. When we ask, "What does this or that signify?" we are asking about two kinds of things, and, in fact, about things which are opposed. In the first place, we call what we are thinking of, the meaning, the end or intention, the general thought of this or that expression, work of art, &c.; if we ask about its intrinsic character, it is essentially the *thought* that is in it of which we wish to have an idea. When we thus ask "What is God?" "What does the expression God signify?" it is the thought involved in it that we desire to know; the idea we possess already. Accordingly, what is signified here is that we have got to specify the Notion, and thus it follows that the *Notion* is the signification; it is the Absolute, the nature of God as grasped by thought, the logical knowledge of this, to which we desire to attain. This, then, is the one signification of signification, and so far, that which we call the Absolute has a meaning identical with the expression God.

b. But we put the question again, in a second sense, according to which it is the opposite of this which is sought after. When we

begin to occupy ourselves with pure thought-determinations, and
not with outward ideas, it may be that the mind does not feel satisfied, is not at home, in these, and asks what this pure thought-
determination signifies. For example, every one can understand for
himself what is meant by the terms unity, objective, subjective, &c.,
and yet it may very well happen that the specific form of thought
we call the unity of subjective and objective, the unity of real and
ideal, is not understood. What is asked for in such a case is the
meaning in the very opposite sense from that which was required
before. Here it is an idea or a pictorial conception of the thought-
determination which is demanded, an example of the content, which
has as yet only been given in thought. If we find a thought-content
difficult to understand, the difficulty lies in this, that we possess no
pictorial idea of it; it is by means of an example that it becomes
clear to us, and that the mind first feels at home with itself in this
content. When, accordingly, we start with the ordinary conception
of God, the Philosophy of Religion has to consider its signification—
this, namely, that God is the Idea, the Absolute, the Essential
Reality which is grasped in thought and in the Notion, and this it
has in common with logical philosophy; the logical Idea is God as
He is in Himself. But it is just the nature of God that He should
not be implicit or in Himself only. He is as essentially for Himself,
the Absolute Spirit, not only the Being who keeps Himself within
thought, but who also manifests Himself, and gives Himself objectivity.

  c. Thus, in contemplating the Idea of God, in the Philosophy of
Religion, we have at the same time to do with the manner of His
manifestation or presentation to us; He simply makes Himself apparent, represents Himself to Himself. This is the aspect of the determinate being or existence of the Absolute. In the Philosophy of
Religion we have thus the Absolute as object; not, however, merely
in the form of thought, but also in the form of its manifestation.
The universal Idea is thus to be conceived of with the purely concrete meaning of essentiality in general, and is to be regarded from
the point of view of its activity in displaying itself, in appearing, in
revealing itself. Popularly speaking, we say God is the Lord of the
natural world and of the realm of Spirit. He *is* the absolute harmony
of the two, and it is He who produces and carries on this harmony.
Here neither thought and Notion nor their manifestation—determinate being or existence—are wanting.

SØREN KIERKEGAARD

God and the Subjective Thinker

Søren Kierkegaard was born in Denmark in 1813; in a relatively short lifetime he wrote the many brilliant works that were to form the basis of existential philosophy. A Christian thinker and an admirer of Socrates, Kierkegaard never tired of arguing for the superiority of the religious and ethical dimensions of human life over against speculative philosophy. Kierkegaard developed his thought at a time when Hegel's philosophy was dominant. Although he admired Hegel's achievement, he repeatedly attacked Hegelian philosophy for ignoring the concrete individual who "exists" in a world of decision and risk, concentrating instead on an impersonal system of cosmic truth. Kierkegaard's chief aim was to reinterpret Christianity as the true "subjectivity." Among his many writings are Philosophical Fragments, *1844;* The Concept of Dread, *1844;* Fear and Trembling, *1843 and* Either-Or, *1843. Kierkegaard died in 1855.*

The most dangerous form of scepticism is always that which least looks like it. The notion that pure thought is the positive truth for an existing individual, is sheer scepticism, for this positiveness is chimerical. It is a glorious thing to be able to explain the past, the whole of human history; but if the ability to understand the past is to be the summit of attainment for a living individual, this positiveness is scepticism, and a dangerous form of it, because of the deceptive quantity of things understood. Hence the terrible thing can happen to Hegel's philosophy, that an indirect attack is most dangerous. Let a doubting youth, an existing doubter, imbued with a lovable and unlimited youthful confidence in a hero of thought, confidingly seek in Hegel's positive philosophy the truth, the truth for existence: he will write a formidable epigram over Hegel. Please do not misunderstand me. I do not mean that every youth can vanquish Hegel, far from it; if the youth is conceited and foolish enough to attempt it, his attack will be without significance. No, the youth must not even think of attacking Hegel. On the contrary, let him submit himself unconditionally, in feminine devotion, but with sufficient vigor of determination to hold fast to his problem: he will

Reprinted with permission of the publisher from *Kierkegaard's Concluding Unscientific Postscript* (1846; trans. David F. Swenson and Walter Lowrie; Princeton: Princeton University Press, 1941), pp. 275–279; 178–179.

become a satirist without suspecting it. The youth is an existing doubter. Hovering in doubt and without a foothold for his life, he reaches out for the truth—in order to exist in it. He is negative and the philosophy of Hegel is positive—what wonder then that he seeks anchorage in Hegel. But a philosophy of pure thought is for an existing individual a chimera, if the truth that is sought is something to exist in. To exist under the guidance of pure thought is like travelling in Denmark with the help of a small map of Europe, on which Denmark shows no larger than a steel pen-point—aye, it is still more impossible. The admiration and enthusiasm of the youth, his boundless confidence in Hegel, is precisely the satire upon Hegel. This is something that would long ago have been perceived, if the prestige of pure thought had not been bolstered by an over-awing opinion, so that people have not dared to say that it is anything but excellent, and to avow that they have understood it—though this last is in a certain sense impossible, since this philosophy cannot help anyone to an understanding of himself, which is surely an absolute condition for all other kinds of understanding. Socrates said quite ironically that he did not know whether he was a human being or something else, but an Hegelian can say with due solemnity in the confessional: "I do not know whether I am a human being—but I have understood the System." I for my part would rather say: "I know that I am a human being, and I know that I have not understood the System." And having said so much quite simply, I will add that if any of our Hegelians will take pity on me and help me to an understanding of the System, there will be nothing in the way of hindrances interposed from my side. I shall strive to make myself as stupid as possible, so as not to have a single presupposition except my ignorance, only in order to be in a position to learn the more; and I shall strive to be as indifferent as possible over against every accusation directed against my lack of scientific training, merely to make sure of learning something.

It is impossible to exist without passion, unless we understand the word "exist" in the loose sense of a so-called existence. Every Greek thinker was therefore essentially a passionate thinker. I have often reflected how one might bring a man into a state of passion. I have thought in this connection that if I could get him seated on a horse and the horse made to take fright and gallop wildly, or better still, for the sake of bringing the passion out, if I could take a man who wanted to arrive at a certain place as quickly as possible, and hence already had some passion, and could set him astride a horse that can scarcely walk—and yet this is what existence is like if one is to become consciously aware of it. Or if a driver were otherwise not especially inclined toward passion, if someone hitched a team of horses to a wagon for him, one of them a Pegasus and the other a worn-out jade, and told him to drive—I think one might succeed. And it is just this that it means to exist, if one is to become conscious of it. Eternity is the winged horse, infinitely fast, and time is a worn-out jade; the existing individual is the driver. That is to say, he is such a driver when his mode of existence is not an existence loosely so called; for then he is no driver, but a drunken peasant who lies asleep in the wagon and lets the horses take care of themselves. To be sure, he also drives and is a driver; and so there are perhaps many who—also exist.

In so far as existence consists in movement there must be something which can give continuity to the movement and hold it together, for otherwise there is no movement. Just as the assertion that everything is true means that nothing is true, so the assertion that everything is in motion means that there is no motion. The unmoved is therefore a constituent of the motion as its measure and its end. Otherwise the assertion that everything is in motion, and, if one also wishes to take time away, that everything is always in motion, is *ipso facto* the assertion of a state of rest. Aristotle, who emphasizes movement in so many ways, therefore says that God, Himself unmoved, moves all. Now while pure thought either abrogates motion altogether, or meaninglessly imports it into logic, the difficulty facing an existing individual is how to give his existence the continuity without which everything simply vanishes. An abstract continuity is no continuity, and the very existence of the existing individual is sufficient to prevent his continuity from having essential stability; while passion gives him a momentary continuity, a continuity which at one and the same time is a restraining influence and a moving impulse. The goal of movement for an existing individual is to arrive at a decision, and to renew it. The eternal is the factor of continuity; but an abstract eternity is extraneous to the movement of life, and a concrete eternity within the existing individual is the maximum degree of his passion. All idealizing passion is an anticipation of the eternal in existence functioning so as to help the individual to exist. The eternity of abstract thought is arrived at by abstracting from existence. The realm of pure thought is a sphere in which the existing individual finds himself only by virtue of a mistaken beginning; and this error revenges itself by making the existence of the individual insignificant, and giving his language a flavor of lunacy. This seems to be the case with almost the entire mass of men in our day, when you rarely or never hear a person speak as if he were an existing individual human being, but rather as one who sees everything in a dizzy pantheistic haze, forever talking about millions and whole nations and the historical evolution. But the passionate anticipation of the eternal is nevertheless not an absolute continuity for the existing individual; but it is the possibility of an approximation to the only true continuity that he can have. Here we are again reminded of my thesis that subjectivity is truth; for an objective truth is like the eternity of abstract thought, extraneous to the movement of existence.

Abstract thought is disinterested, but for an existing individual, existence is the highest interest. . . . Pure thought is altogether detached, and not like the abstract thought which does indeed abstract from existence, but nevertheless preserves a relationship to it. This pure thought, hovering in mystic suspension between heaven and earth and emancipated from every relation to an existing individual, explains everything in its own terms but fails to explain itself. It explains everything in such fashion that no decisive explanation of the essential question becomes possible. Thus when an existing individual asks about the relationship between pure thought and an existing individual, pure thought makes no reply, but merely explains existence within pure thought and so confuses everything. It assigns to existence, the category upon which pure thought must suffer shipwreck, a place within pure thought itself; in this fashion everything that is said about existence is essentially revoked. When pure thought speaks of the immediate unity of reflection-in-self and reflection-in-other, and says that this immediate unity is abrogated, something must of course intervene so as to divide the two phases of this immediate unity. What can this something be? It is time. But time cannot find a place within pure thought. What then is the meaning of the talk about abrogation and transition and the new unity? And in general, what does it mean to think in such a manner as merely to pretend to think, because everything that is said is absolutely revoked? And what is the meaning of the refusal to admit that one thinks in this manner, constantly blazoning forth this pure thought as positive truth?

Just as existence has combined thought and existence by making the existing individual a thinker, so there are two media: the medium of abstract thought, and the medium of reality. But pure thought is still a third medium, quite recently discovered. It therefore begins, as the saying is, after the most exhaustive abstraction. The relation which abstract thought still sustains to that from which it abstracts, is something which pure thought innocently or thoughtlessly ignores. Here is rest for every doubt, here is the eternal positive truth, and whatever else one may be pleased to say. That is, pure thought is a phantom. If the Hegelian philosophy has emancipated itself from every presupposition, it has won this freedom by means of one lunatic postulate: the initial transition to pure thought. . . .

Let us take as an example the knowledge of God. Objectively, reflection is directed to the problem of whether this object is the true God; subjectively, reflection is directed to the question whether the individual is related to a something *in such a manner* that his relationship is in truth a God-relationship. On which side is the truth now to be found? Ah, may we not here resort to a mediation, and say: It is on neither side, but in the mediation of both? Excellently well said, provided we might have it explained how an existing individual manages to be in a state of mediation. For to be in a state of mediation is to be finished, while to exist is to become. Nor can an existing individual be in two places at the same time—he cannot be an identity of subject and object. When he is nearest to being in two places at the same time he is in passion; but passion is momentary, and passion is also the highest expression of subjectivity.

The existing individual who chooses to pursue the objective way enters upon the entire approximation-process by which it is proposed to bring God to light objectively. But this is in all eternity impossible, because God is a subject, and therefore exists only for subjectivity in inwardness. The existing individual who chooses the subjective way apprehends instantly the entire dialectical difficulty involved in having to use some time, perhaps a long time, in finding God objectively; and he feels this dialectical difficulty in all its painfulness, because every moment is wasted in which he does not have

God.[1] That very instant he has God, not by virtue of any objective deliberation, but by virtue of the infinite passion of inwardness. The objective inquirer, on the other hand, is not embarrassed by such dialectical difficulties as are involved in devoting an entire period of investigation to finding God—since it is possible that the inquirer may die tomorrow; and if he lives he can scarcely regard God as something to be taken along if convenient, since God is precisely that which one takes *a tout prix*, which in the understanding of passion constitutes the true inward relationship to God.

[1] In this manner God certainly becomes a postulate, but not in the otiose manner in which this word is commonly understood. It becomes clear rather that the only way in which an existing individual comes into relation with God, is when the dialectical contradiction brings his passion to the point of despair, and helps him to embrace God with the "category of despair" (faith). Then the postulate is so far from being arbitrary that it is precisely a life-necessity. It is then not so much that God is a postulate, as that the existing individual's postulation of God is a necessity.

ALFRED NORTH WHITEHEAD

Religion and Metaphysics

Religion requires a metaphysical backing; for its authority is endangered by the intensity of the emotions which it generates. Such emotions are evidence of some vivid experience; but they are a very poor guarantee for its correct interpretation.

Thus dispassionate criticism of religious belief is beyond all things necessary. The foundations of dogma must be laid in a rational metaphysics which criticises meanings, and endeavours to express the most general concepts adequate for the all-inclusive universe.

This position has never been seriously doubted, though in practice it is often evaded. One of the most serious periods of neglect occurred in the middle of the nineteenth century, through the dominance of the historical interest.

It is a curious delusion that the rock upon which our beliefs can be founded is an historical investigation. You can only interpret the past in terms of the present. The present is all that you have; and unless in this present you can find general principles which interpret the present as including a representation of the whole community of existents, you cannot move a step beyond your little patch of immediacy.

Thus history presupposes a metaphysic. It can be objected that we believe in the past and talk about it without settling our metaphysical principles. That is certainly the case. But you can only deduce metaphysical dogmas from your interpretation of the past on the basis of a prior metaphysical interpretation of the present.[1]

In so far as your metaphysical beliefs are implicit, you vaguely interpret the past on the lines of the present. But when it comes to the primary metaphysical data, the world of which you are immediately conscious is the whole datum.

This criticism applies equally to a science or to a religion which hopes to justify itself without any appeal to metaphysics. The dif-

[1] By "metaphysics" I mean the science which seeks to discover the general ideas which are indispensably relevant to the analysis of everything that happens.

ference is that religion is the longing of the spirit that the facts of existence should find their justification in the nature of existence. "My soul thirsteth for God," writes the Psalmist.

But science can leave its metaphysics implicit and retire behind our belief in the pragmatic value of its general descriptions. If religion does that, it admits that its dogmas are merely pleasing ideas for the purpose of stimulating its emotions. Science (at least as a temporary methodological device) can rest upon a naïve faith; religion is the longing for justification. When religion ceases to seek for penetration, for clarity, it is sinking back into its lower forms. The ages of faith are the ages of rationalism.

In the previous lectures religious experience was considered as a fact. It consists of a certain widespread, direct apprehension of a character exemplified in the actual universe. Such a character includes in itself certain metaphysical presuppositions. In so far as we trust the objectivity of the religious intuitions, to that extent we must also hold that the metaphysical doctrines are well founded.

It is for this reason that in the previous lecture the broadest view of religious experience was insisted on. If, at this stage of thought, we include points of radical divergence between the main streams, the whole evidential force is indefinitely weakened. Thus religious experience cannot be taken as contributing to metaphysics any direct evidence for a personal God in any sense transcendent or creative.

The universe, thus disclosed, is through and through interdependent. The body pollutes the mind, the mind pollutes the body. Physical energy sublimates itself into zeal; conversely, zeal stimulates the body. The biological ends pass into ideals of standards, and the formation of standards affects the biological facts. The individual is formative of the society, the society is formative of the individual. Particular evils infect the whole world, particular goods point the way of escape.

The world is at once a passing shadow and a final fact. The shadow is passing into the fact, so as to be constitutive of it; and yet the fact is prior to the shadow. There is a kingdom of heaven prior to the actual passage of actual things, and there is the same kingdom finding its completion through the accomplishment of this passage.

But just as the kingdom of heaven transcends the natural world, so does this world transcend the kingdom of heaven. For the world is evil, and the kingdom is good. The kingdom is in the world, and yet not of the world.

The actual world, the world of experiencing, and of thinking, and of physical activity, is a community of many diverse entities; and these entities contribute to, or derogate from, the common value of the total community. At the same time, these actual entities are, for themselves, their own value, individual and separable. They add to the common stock and yet they suffer alone. The world is a scene of solitariness in community.

The individuality of entities is just as important as their community. The topic of religion is individuality in community.

JOHN E. SMITH

The Encounter Between
Philosophy and Religion

The editor was born in 1921 and received his doctorate from Columbia University. He has taught at Vassar College, Barnard College, and since 1952 at Yale University. He is the author of Royce's Social Infinite (1950), The Spirit of American Philosophy (1963), *and is editor of Jonathan Edwards'* Treatise Concerning Religious Affections (1959).

Religious faith and philosophical thought, the most fundamental spiritual forms in human life, have always found themselves in the peculiar position of not being able to get along with each other and of not being able to remain permanently apart. Their overlap of interest, as shown in their common concern for such matters as the ultimate nature of things, the form of the good life, the destiny of man and his status in the universe, has led to their mutual involvement. At times the two have developed together in fruitful cooperation and mutual support, at times they have eyed each other with infinite suspicion born of the fear that each seeks to supplant the other. As regards their cooperation, it has been shown that religious thought can develop most successfully through the medium of concepts and categories furnished by philosophical investigation, and that philosophy proves to be most original and vital when it is directed toward those ultimate questions about the universe and human life which religion keeps continually before us. The tradition of Christian Platonism, for example, and the great synthesis achieved by Thomas Aquinas show the power and depth of theology when it has philosophical form and self-consciousness; the great philosophers, on the other hand, have been those who concerned themselves with the most fundamental metaphysical questions that have always bordered on the religious concern.

Though the two forms may work together, we must not forget that their relations have also been marked by serious tensions. Philosophical minds have often regarded religion as superstition and as an easy road to conclusions about nature, man, and God which,

From John E. Smith, *Reason and God* (New Haven: Yale University Press, 1961), pp. ix–xiv. Reprinted with the permission of the Yale University Press.

if justified at all, can be attained only as a result of long and pains-taking argument. Religious thinkers have sometimes looked upon philosophy as a blasphemous exaltation of human reason which leads man to venture into regions reserved exclusively for revelation. Every form of philosophical nihilism, materialism, and positivism expresses the suspicion from the philosophical side. Pietism, ecclesiastical dogmatism, and fideism give voice to the suspicion from the religious side. Where either side has prevailed, the inevitable result has been some form of fanaticism and the sealing off of the different aspects of human experience from interchange with one another.

It has been characteristic of the Western tradition that one or the other of these basic outlooks has dominated at a given time. We think, for example, of the Greco-Roman world as a time when the ideas of the great philosophers prevailed and of the Middle Ages as a period under the sway of religion. This seesaw relationship has given rise to the impression that the connections between them belong to the accidents of history and that there is no inner truth of the matter. Nothing could be more erroneous. Our experience of the long interplay between the philosophical traditions initiated by the thinkers of the ancient world and the schools of Christian theology shows that there is an intrinsic connection between the philosophical enterprise and religious faith. This connection, paradoxically enough, becomes most clearly apparent when atttempts are made to hold the two entirely apart. Experience has taught us that religion is in constant danger of falling into superstition, dogmatism, and obscurantism unless it encounters philosophical criticism and becomes related to other facets of cultural life. Whether this criticism comes from without, in the form of a philosophy that seeks to interpret religious affirmations in critical terms, or from within, in the form of a theology sensitive to philosophical considerations, it remains true that religion, left to its own internal devices, tends to be self-indulgent and to insulate itself from critical contact with culture and knowledge gained from so-called secular sources.

Philosophy, on the other hand, is not free from complacency. Without the goad of religion and its focus on the ultimate problems of human existence, philosophers tend to retire into technical corners of their own and to concentrate exclusively on questions of methodology and formal expression. Discussion about how one *would* go about dealing with a given issue, or prescriptions concerning the form that the results *would* take, have an endless fascination for philosophical minds, especially when they are free from concern for the urgency of the concrete problems themselves. Religious experience and insight highlight concrete problems of human existence and continually draw thoughtful men to their consideration. The religious dimension of human life provides philosophy with endless material for its own speculation. When philosophy loses touch with religion, there is the great risk of formalization, so that ultimate questions are postponed and preliminary questions gradually come to occupy the whole ground.

For many reasons intimately connected with the far-reaching social and cultural developments of the past two hundred years, philosophy and religious thought have grown steadily apart. As a result of the critical examination of reason and the skeptical conclusions that followed, philosophy was forced to renounce its competence and then its right to deal with classical metaphysical problems and the related issues posed by religious belief. Religion became for many a wholly practical affair, to be allied with morality or art but separated from philosophy and science. The divorce has had the most deep-seated consequences for both sides, and the present intellectual situation presents us with a clear picture of the end result. The scale of philosophy has been greatly reduced; direct confrontation of speculative questions has given way to largely technical questions of procedure and to the formalization of previous results; the search for new philosophical ideas has often been abandoned in favor of attempts to find clearer ways of stating old conclusions. From the other side, religion has found itself separated from rational justification; it has been tempted to retreat within the confines of its own community, to reject all critical discussion with the cultural forms in which it exists, and to base itself so completely upon "commitment" that it appears devoid of all rational compulsion. Some spokesmen for religion speak as though religious doctrines become suspect just to the extent to which it appears possible to give rational justification for them.

Another factor leading to the present situation has been the phenomenal development of the natural sciences. At the same time that philosophers were abandoning their classical province of metaphysics, the natural sciences were establishing themselves as the final arbiters of all questions of fact and existence. Philosophers themselves were fascinated by this development, and many sought to become part of it through the reconstruction of philosophy with science as a basis. Various forms of scientific philosophy developed, and the important total outcome was the exclusive rooting of philosophical thought in the highly abstract conclusions of the sciences. Quite apart from the many issues raised by this turn of affairs, philosophy slipped into a one-sided dependence on science to the *exclusion* of other aspects of man's total experience such as religion and art.

Of vital importance to the cultural life of the present time is a renewal of the ancient encounter between philosophy and religion. The essays that follow are aimed at bringing about such a renewal by focusing on crucial questions that arise when religion and philosophy meet—the relations between Christianity and philosophy, the possibility of natural theology and the relation of religion to experience, the problem of a morality completely separated from religious foundations, the nature of religious symbolism and the bearing of a sacramental conception of the universe upon the expression of a poetic vision. Over and above specific issues, there is the matter of a basic self-understanding; the true nature of religion and philosophy is most clearly revealed in mutual encounter, and aspects of each that are often hidden or thrust into the background become manifest.

Religion is instituted by and continues to draw its life from the initial certainties arising from the experiences of its founders and heroes. Consequently, to proceed from the religious side means not so much the seeking after a truth yet undiscovered as the proclaiming of the meaning and importance of a truth already found. Philosophy, on the other hand, is born from wonder and from the quest of reason to find a pattern, a wisdom in things which is still to be disclosed. One side sets out from certainties; the other seeks to arrive at them. Viewed immediately, each side has its own distinctive and dominant character. This character, however, is not exhaustive; each side has within itself, as a kind of recessive element, the distinctive characteristic of the other, a similarity that becomes fully realized only when the two encounter each other; genuine encounter means that each enterprise is forced to a new level of self-consciousness. Religion discovers that its life is not exclusively a matter of certainties which exclude doubt and the rational quest; philosophy discovers that its life is not exclusively a search, because the rational quest itself must be carried out against a background of truths taken for granted and never fully justified in the course of any inquiry. Philosophy, moreover, comes to its own certainties when it comes to express its constructive results.

Religion becomes a stagnant, lifeless affair if all doubt and questing are removed from it. In the encounter with philosophy the meaning of faith as a continual incorporation and overcoming of doubt is revealed. Philosophy, in turn, becomes a sterile formalism when it takes itself to be no more than a way of attacking problems, a method for conducting an inquiry. The encounter with religion forces an acknowledgment of the certainties which all philosophies harbor in themselves, even if their proponents claim that they have no fixed conclusions and are merely humble seekers after truth. No philosopher has been able to avoid assumptions and no one has ever succeeded in doubting everything consistently. The encounter of philosophy with religion shows, in short, that religion cannot be all finding and that philosophy cannot be all seeking.

Bibliography

Barth, Karl. *Evangelical Theology: An Introduction.* New York: Holt, 1963. [An expanded version of lectures given by Barth during a tour of America. The book is important because it expresses the extreme view that there is no way of comprehending the Christian God from a philosophical standpoint.]

Bertocci, Peter A. *Introduction to the Philosophy of Religion.* New York: Prentice-Hall, 1951. [An introduction to the problems of the philosophy of religion with special emphasis on the argument for God through purpose or design.]

Buber, Martin. *The Eclipse of God.* New York: Harper, 1952. [A series of essays on the relation between religion and contemporary culture. Among the topics discussed are existentialism, Jungian psychology, and the relation of religion to morality.]

Gilson, Etienne. *God and Philosophy.* New Haven: Yale Univ. Press, 1941. [A classic brief account of the history of western thought with emphasis upon the relation between the Judeo-Christian idea of God and the dominant philosophical doctrines. Gilson follows in the tradition of Thomas Aquinas.]

Hartshorne, Charles. *The Logic of Perfection.* La Salle, Ill.: Open Court, 1962. [An intricate interpretation of the Ontological Argument focusing on the idea of perfection. This book forms the basis of Boyce Gibson's discussion of the two ideas of God.]

Hick, John. *Faith and Knowledge.* Ithaca: Cornell Univ. Press, 1957. [A discussion representing the viewpoint of philosophical analysis. It shows the manner in which the analytic approach in philosophy can be combined with confessional theology.]

James, E. O. *The Concept of Deity.* London: Hutchinson's Univ. Library, 1950. [An historical and philosophical study of the main ideas of God that have developed in the history of religion, East and West.]

Van der Leeuw, G. *Religion in Essence and Manifestation.* J. E. Turner (trans.). London: Allen & Unwin, 1938. [Contains a mine of information about religious experience and its facets. The book should be used as a companion piece to metaphysical interpretations of religion.]

Otto, Rudolf. *The Idea of the Holy.* J. W. Harvey (trans.). London: Oxford Univ. Press, 1923. [A classic analysis of the nonrational side of religious experience. The mystical element in religion is well treated.]

Ramsey, Ian T. *Religious Language.* London: SCM Press Ltd., 1957. [An excellent introduction to the contemporary approach to the philosophy of religion through the analysis of religious language and its "logic."]

Tillich, Paul. *Dynamics of Faith.* New York: Harper, 1957. [A lucid account of the nature of religious faith, the symbols in which it is expressed and the problem of religious truth.]

Wild, John. *Human Freedom and Social Order.* Durham: Duke Univ. Press, 1959. [A spirited defense of Christian philosophy as the proper solution to the problem of relating theology and philosophy.]

DATE DUE

DEC 1 3 1991		
APR 1 4 1995		
SEP 1 9 1997		
MAR 1 6 1998		

HIGHSMITH 45-220

95049